Responding to A

Abide Counseling Press

Sarah McDugal
Jennifer Jill Schwirzer
Nicole Parker

SAFE CHURCHES - RESPONDING TO ABUSE WITHIN THE FAITH COMMUNITY

©2019 Sarah McDugal, Jennifer Jill Schwirzer, and Nicole Parker

Published by Abide Counseling Press

Visit the authors websites at:

http://ProjectSafeChurch.com

http://SarahMcDugal.com

http://JenniferJill.org

http://HeartThirst.com

First Printing: September 2019

ISBN: 978-1-7334834-1-4

Cover Design by: Emmalee Shallenberger

Emmalee Designs

http://EmmaleeDesignsArt.com

Facebook: @EmmaleeDesignsArt

Interior Design by: Kyla Steinkraus

Bible Verses quoted are from NKJV (Chapters 1-4,7) and NLT (Chapters 5-6, 8-9)

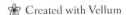 Created with Vellum

OTHER WORKS

Sarah McDugal

One Face: Shed the Mask, Own Your Values, and Lead Wisely

Myths We Believe, Predators We Trust: 37 Things You Don't Want to Know About Abuse In Church (But You Should)

Jennifer Jill Schwirzer

Damsel Arise!

13 Weeks to Peace: Allow Jesus to Heal Your Heart and Mind

13 Weeks to Love: Allow Jesus to Heal Your Relationships

13 Weeks to Joy: How to Hold the Happiness God Gives

Twice Upon A Time: The David Asscherick and Nathan Renner Story

A Gospel Story

Finding My Way in Milwaukee

A Light for the Last Days

Dying to be Beautiful: Help, Hope, and Healing for Eating Disorders

A Deep but Dazzling Darkness: Exploring God's "Dark Side" in the light of His Love

I Want it All: A Teen Devotional

A Most Precious Message: My Personal Discovery of Liberating Joy in the Gospel of Jesus

Testimony of a Seeker: A Young Woman's Journey to Grace

Nicole Parker

Faith Roots: A Story of God's Trustworthy Love for Children of All Ages

Humble Stones: A Story of God's Self-Sacrificing Love for Children of All Ages

Sanctuary Light: A Story of God's Redeeming Love for Children of All Ages

To be released:

Wings of Love: A Story of God's Just and Merciful Love for Children of All Ages

Joseph's Bones: A Story of God's Triumphant Love for Children of All Ages

CONTENTS

To
the voiceless ones

ACKNOWLEDGMENTS

This book would not be complete without an expression of gratitude to Martin Fancher, Nicholas Miller, Alan Parker, Haskell Williams, and the many other fierce leaders with even fiercer hearts, who are determined to stand for the right, act with courage, and defend the vulnerable.

To the families who have affirmed our sanity, the girlfriends who have had our backs, and the prayer warriors who have lifted up our hands like Aaron and Hur flanking Moses above the battlefield...feeble words are not thanks enough.

And to the survivors of abuse within the church, who exhibit the greatest courage of all—telling the truth whether it is in a whisper or a shout, even when they are repaid only in slander and disdain—the ones who keep on living, and healing, and breaking the cycles of generational pain. You are the real heroes among us. You are our reason.

INTRODUCTION

"You shall not afflict any widow or fatherless child. If you afflict them in any way, and they cry at all to Me, I will surely hear their cry; and My wrath will become hot, and I will kill you with the sword." Exodus 22:22-24, NKJV (Unless otherwise noted, all Scripture in this book will be from the New King James Version.)

Who Are We?

This book is the result of a gospel-driven strategic partnership created to protect victims of sexual and other abuses. Our alliance was formed largely to streamline the process of guiding church leaders through the process of confronting sexual abuse biblically, thus creating the best possible environment for helping both victims and perpetrators heal.

Initially, our efforts were focused on developing a system by which we could guide those who report sexual abuse through the process of bringing reports to the attention of those who could help prevent further such abuse—namely, church leaders and/or law enforcement. However, we quickly realized that the majority of church members and leaders who cared deeply about abuse were simply not educated on biblical processes of handling sexual abuse situations—or abuse in general. Many sincere members and leaders were unaware of state and federal legal requirements for specific kinds of mandated reporting, and were lacking basic skills needed for assessing and responding to situations in ways that would bring healing. This led us to launch educational efforts and create resources that would equip godly, sincere defenders everywhere to know how to process abuse better.

While our work focuses specifically on sexual abuse situations, most of the principles outlined in this book and our other resources are also applicable to a broad spectrum of abuse situations. Accordingly, we have not focused narrowly in this book on sexual abuse only, but have sought to explain principles that apply to all forms of abuse. In this book, we generally refer to abusers as "he" and victims as "she" for the sake of simplicity and ease of reading, but we do realize that females may be abusers, and males may be victims.

Why Do We Do This Work?

As with every truly transformative movement, the motivation behind our work is the gospel—bringing salvation to the people Jesus died to save. Abuse is one of Satan's most effective tools in driving people away from faith in a God of love. Abuse roars in the ear of the victim, "Where was God's everlasting love when this happened? Where was His mighty power to save?" Abuse thus becomes one of the most powerful arguments in favor of self-reliance and self-centeredness.

In other words, unless handled biblically, abuse powerfully tempts survivors to sin in response to being sinned against. God is angry at sin, and a certain righteous anger can (and should!) lead us to rise up against injustice in order to vindicate God's character. However, mishandled anger can easily lead to sin simply metastasizing in the lives of everyone involved. "Be angry, and do not sin" is the biblical injunction. It is only with a careful balance of justice and mercy that the character of God can be reflected in a correct balance, and there is never a more important time to reflect this balance than when handling abuse situations.

The absence of righteous wrath being poured out in response to unjust suffering is a central argument in most atheists' reasoning that there can be no loving God ruling the universe. In order to bring non-Christians to the foot of the cross, as well as to restore victims' belief in a God of love, the church must demonstrate the character of a loving God. Practically, that means we must demonstrate that we care when evil people ravage innocent victims.

We must display the delicate balance of justice and mercy reflected not only in the tenderhearted Jesus of the New Testament, but also in the mighty God of the Old Testament, who repeatedly unveils His mighty arm to defend His people and stand up to evil oppressors. Finally, we must care enough about abusers to do all we can to follow the biblical process of consequences, not out of blind rage, but out of genuine desire to bring them to repentance, if possible. We must become "wise as serpents and harmless as doves" (Matthew 10:16). To do these things, we must seek the wisdom given to Solomon in answer to prayer. We must trust that God will give it to those humble enough in heart to realize their need, and willing enough to step into uncomfortable situations in order to "do right because it is right" (*Christ's Object Lessons*, p. 97).

It was out of this vision that this book was created: a resource to help guide godly defenders through the process of applying principles of redemption in the wisest ways possible, for the work of redemption. The goals of this book are dual: 1) To equip defenders to help survivors heal, and 2) to equip victims themselves to heal and become empowered as defenders and healers.

What Exactly *Is* Abuse, Anyway?

Abuse is all about power. "I will ascend above the heights of the clouds, I will be like the Most High" (Isaiah 14:14) was Lucifer's defiant cry. He wanted to be like the Highest--but only in power, not in character. In some way, the spirit of self-exaltation has been reflected in every sinful thought and action since. Abuse is perhaps the clearest reflection of the power-hungry character of Satan. In contrast, the heart of God is tenderest toward those who are hurting and weak. "A bruised reed He will not break" (Isaiah 42:3). Pure and undefiled religion leads God's true followers to care for the most vulnerable of society (James 1:27). When we see wounded and vulnerable people, our heart impulse will be to protect and nurture them.

Conversely, abuse is rooted in a desire to exalt self by crushing down others. The true follower of Jesus instinctively protects tender little children, but the child abuser sees vulnerability as an opportunity to exploit. Abusers often strategically evaluate for months, like wolves looking for a weak sheep they can separate from the flock. While abuse takes many forms, the central characteristic that distinguishes it from other forms of sin is that it results from a hardening of the heart against the Holy Spirit. The amount of hardening of the heart that has happened must be evaluated prayerfully by those who are trying to help, because abusers often will not heal or change in response to anything except painful consequences (such as a prolonged loss of power over others). One of the most common mistakes made in dealing with abuse situations is quickly assuming that abusers have repented, without waiting to discern carefully whether the fruits of repentance are being consistently manifested. Achan confessions that are forced out by discovery mean very little in God's eyes.

"In the last days perilous times will come: For men will be lovers of themselves..." (2 Timothy 3:1, 2). These verses and the ones immediately after them identify a string of factors that are clearly tied to abuse. If we believe the biblical description of the end of time, we must acknowledge that abuse will be a central end-time issue. How is it possible for it not to be so? Self-exaltation—the thirst for power over others—is the root of all abuse. And it will not merely be a problem outside of the church, for Paul finishes this description of end-time sinners by summarizing it as "having a form of godliness but denying its power" (2 Timothy 3:5). It may be hard to imagine the sort of evils described by Paul as flourishing in God's church, but when dealing with abuse, we see the ugliest underbelly of hypocrisy within the church. As we will discuss, abuse disfigures victims' picture of the character of God, thus seriously hindering their ability to form a relationship with Him. This makes it a central evangelistic issue.

Abuse is also usually the result of advanced sin against the Holy Spirit. This means that confronting abusers will be difficult, and sometimes even dangerous. However, we must never decide whether we want to do God's bidding based on whether it is risky, hard or painful.

Should Confronting Abuse Be a High Priority at the End of Time?

"This is a distraction from God's work," one pastor complained when a reporter of sexual abuse asked for his cooperation in dealing with an abuser in his congregation. "How much time do I have to waste on this before I can get back to fulfilling the Great Commission?"

Certainly, dealing biblically with abuse situations can be messy. However, most quality discipleship and evangelistic work is time-consuming. Jesus didn't hesitate to tackle issues merely because they would cause hassles for Him—for example, He fearlessly stood up against the abusers of the woman caught in adultery. Repeatedly, He made a point of confronting those who treated weak or disadvantaged people badly.

Throughout the Old Testament, abuse of the vulnerable (such as orphans or widows) was one of the two most serious sins God promised to punish. (The other was idolatry, which is another underlying factor in every abuse situation.) In some cases, rape was the only crime that was to be given the death penalty on the testimony of only one witness—the woman who had been raped (Deuteronomy 22:25-27). God even warned that those who refused to deal justly with rapists should themselves receive the death penalty (Judges 19 and 20).

Abuse profoundly misrepresents the character of God. Confronting abuse is a crucial part of restoring the victims' picture of the character of God, as well as of exemplifying God's character to a world longing to see true love. Far from being a distraction from God's work, this is a central part of the character of Christ being reproduced in His people, so that He can come to claim us as His own (*Christ's Object Lessons,* p. 69).

When the church mishandles abuse, *we* participate in profoundly misrepresenting the character of God. By portraying God as something other than loving, we actually drive people away from relationship with Him, and slander the character of God before unbelievers. But the converse is also true. When the church handles abuse wisely and in love, we present a powerful argument in favor of the God of love— one in which observers cannot help seeing the beauty of God's justice and mercy combined.

Chapter one begins this book with a parable based on many stories we have heard and handled. Whatever happens, let us learn from this false shepherd, so scenarios like this are never reenacted in the churches under our leadership.

THE WOLF AMONG THE SHEEP

I t was a glorious afternoon for a walk. A woman strolled down a sunny lane, enjoying the stunning wildflowers, while a nearby shepherd sat on a sun-warmed stone, reading a book aloud. His contented sheep grazed all around him. Some sheep had settled on the grass near his feet, peacefully snoozing away the afternoon.

Then the woman noticed something horrifying. A wolf had cornered a lamb on the far side of a bush away from the shepherd. The lamb was cringing into the bush, trying to escape, but the wolf was eagerly snapping at its throat.

The woman screamed, startling the wolf, which galloped away. She pulled the lamb from the bush and tenderly examined it, relieved she had come just in time. However, she looked up to see the wolf loping calmly back toward the herd of sheep.

"Hey, look out!" the woman shouted to the shepherd. "There's a wolf coming toward your sheep!" With the lamb in her arms, she ran to the shepherd, who leaped to his feet. "Here's a lamb he almost attacked," she panted, setting the uninjured lamb down at the shepherd's feet. "I saw him corner this lamb over there behind the bush and—"

"Oh, there's no need for concern," the shepherd smiled, watching the wolf slip into the herd of sheep. "That guy right there? He's one of my flock."

The wolf grinned at the woman and slyly grabbed a mouthful of grass.

"What do you mean?" the woman gasped. "I just saw him trying to kill one of your lambs!"

The shepherd picked up the lamb and examined it. "I don't see any blood."

"I got there just in time," the woman explained. "I shouted and the wolf ran away. But I clearly saw him with his teeth bared, about to bite the lamb."

The shepherd smiled benevolently. "So, you mean the lamb wasn't even injured? That means there's nothing to worry about."

The woman stared at him. "That's a wolf, walking around right now with your flock." She pointed at the wolf. "I just saw him behaving as wolves do. He separated a lamb from the flock, got it behind a bush where you couldn't see it, and was about to devour it. Why does that not matter to you?"

The shepherd shrugged, the benevolent smile still on his face. "He's a good friend of mine. He is one of the most faithful members of the flock! I can always count on him to lock up the sheepfold, to be there to wash the dishes after potluck, and to even teach lambs Scripture songs! He's there every week when I herd the flock into the fold. I don't know what I would do without him."

"He's a wolf," the woman said evenly. "Have you ever thought of the reasons he might want to be faithful in going to the sheepfold with your sheep? That's where he mingles with them. That's where he identifies which sheep are vulnerable. He's teaching your lambs Scripture songs?! Don't you realize that's how he gains their trust, and the trust of their parents? I bet he spends his Wednesday nights playing Follow the Leader and Hide-and-Seek with them, too!"

"What if he does? We're just grateful for his burden for the youth!" the shepherd said, his benevolent smile evaporating. "He's a wonderful guy—prays such beautiful prayers, you should hear them. You can't tell me he's a wolf unless you have two or three witnesses to an actual attack."

The woman retorted, "How often does anyone see sexual abuse happen? God knows how hidden these things are. In Deuteronomy 22:25-27, the Bible says that if a man rapes a betrothed woman in the countryside, where she cries out but no one hears, the man will be held guilty. That would make her the only human witness testifying to the rape."

"Are you saying that one rape accusation is enough to convict the accused?" the shepherd asked

"No, because false accusations are another form of abuse, and we must guard against that," the woman replied. "But in the case of the betrothed woman, there would most often be physical evidence, too. This also counts as a 'witness.' Plus, a thorough investigation would likely produce other corroborating evidence. But for the law to require more than one human witness to a rape would not have made sense, as rape almost always happens in secret."

The shepherd shrugged. "I didn't get training in that, so I leave it to the experts! My job is just to get the sheep into the sheepfold every day. And also," he straightened a little taller, "I am called to seek out sheep who are not of this fold, and bring them in."

The woman's eyes widened. "So many sheep have been attacked by wolves in previous herds of sheep! That's why many are out in the fields alone. When they tell the shepherds, they are told that there must be witnesses. But that's the very nature of wolves, to separate their prey from the herd and then attack. That's why—"

"I don't have time for this," the shepherd interrupted, sitting back down on his rock. "You have no idea how busy I am! I have committees and meetings and so many responsibilities involved in getting the sheep into the fold every week. I am reading Scripture to the sheep right now, and I need to get back to it." He began reading loudly, "He shall feed His flock like a shepherd..."

"Please, you've GOT to care enough to protect your sheep!" the woman begged. "What do you think a sheepfold is for—it's for protection from wolves! If anything, your FIRST job is to keep the wolves out!"

"Now listen here!" the shepherd growled. "I've already told you, I'm not an expert on wolves. My job is to look after sheep!"

"Your JOB is to protect your sheep!" the woman stated. "Here!" She reached into her backpack. "I have books that can help you become an expert in identifying wolves! This one is *Predators* by Anna Salter. And here's *Seducers Among Our Children*, by Patrick Crough—that's one written specifically for shepherds, about identifying wolves in the midst of their sheep. Please—just read these, and you can protect your sheep." She held out the books pleadingly. "Haven't you heard? Research shows that the average wolf has fifty to one hundred and fifty victims before the wolf-catchers first catch him—and many more after that."

"I told you, I'm busy," the shepherd replied, shoving the books back at her. "And he is a friend of mine. I'm sure if he were a wolf, I would be able to tell without any books. I'd just know it. I'd feel it, smell it—something."

"You say that because you want to believe it," the woman protested. "We all want to live in a world where if someone were a wolf, we'd just be able to tell magically. But we don't! That's why we must be vigilant in listening when sheep come to us with their stories!"

She looked over at the wolf, which was now prowling around the edge of the flock, eyeing a lamb that had been separated from the flock. She watched as the wolf sidled between the lamb and its mother, and then began edging toward the lamb, propelling it away from the flock. She seized the shepherd by the arm and dragged him to his feet. "Watch this, right now. See what that wolf is doing? That's how wolves behave! You may not be able to tell just by looking at him, but look at how he is separating the lamb from its mother, drawing it out into the prairie grass. We've got to stop him! Get over there!"

The shepherd trotted over to the wolf and had a brief conversation with him. The lamb returned to the flock, and the shepherd returned to the woman, beaming. "I talked with him. He was just taking the lamb out for a walk so he could teach it some Scripture songs."

The woman looked at the shepherd in open-mouthed disbelief. "That's what he told you?"

"You people always want to think the worst of everyone," the shepherd snarled, clearly angry that the woman thought he was naïve. "I believe in following the Bible, where it says to think the BEST of people, not the worst, like YOU do."

"You realize, you're killing sheep." The words just spilled out of the woman's mouth.

"No, I'm not!" the shepherd defended hotly. "There are wolves out there somewhere on the plain. I'm keeping them away from my herd!"

"But you must realize, that doesn't matter when YOU'VE GOT A WOLF IN YOUR HERD!" the woman shouted. "Don't you know that this is the wolf's favorite way of attacking? They hardly ever come after a sheep out of the blue. Sheep run to the herd when they see a wolf coming. The wolves have learned a much easier way, where they don't have to chase, and there's always plenty to eat. By far the most effective way to keep their stomachs full is to live in the midst of the sheep, mingling with them, gaining their trust. Then they single out the vulnerable ones, one by one, and take them off into secluded places to attack. Please, you've got to listen to me! Your sheep are dying while you turn your back!"

"He's part of my flock!" the shepherd shouted. "I'm responsible for him! What if there's a one percent chance that he's innocent?"

"What about the ninety-nine percent chance that he's guilty?" the woman slapped her forehead. "You're a shepherd! It's your job to protect the flock! And how can you do evangelism, and lure more sheep into your fold supposedly for safety from wolves, when YOU'VE GOT A WOLF RIGHT HERE?! Why does this not matter to you?"

"Fine," the shepherd said. "Fine! Bring me two or three sheep who have been wounded by the wolf. Let them tell me about it themselves, in their own words. In the mouth of two or three witnesses—"

"I've been wounded by the wolf," a nearby ewe spoke up, her voice trembling. "I told the last shepherd, but he said I needed to just pray and forgive him."

The shepherd sat silently for a moment, apparently stunned by this revelation of multiple assaults.

"I know a couple of others who also were his victims," the ewe added hesitantly. "But they were too ashamed to tell the shepherd. I don't know if they would even come forward now. Other sheep have been sent away from the flock for coming forward about wolves, or their lives are made miserable; it happens often. The shepherd had told us not to go into the bushes, but the wolf lured us there. He said it was to learn Scripture songs and have prayer with him. But we had disobeyed the shepherd going there, so we knew we would be in trouble. Sheep get sent away, or told to be quiet and forgive; wolves almost never get sent away or reported."

"Do you have any bleeding wounds now?" the shepherd asked.

"No. There's nothing bleeding now; that was years ago. All I have are scars, and most of them are emotional—I can't show them to you. I can only tell you about how everything in my life changed after—"

"I'm not able to take your word unless you can bring me real evidence," the shepherd responded. "Show me something I can see with my eyes! A sheep must be missing a leg before I will believe that my friend is a wolf. Or bring me a carcass. And I need two or three witnesses," he added as an afterthought. "I can't take the word of one sheep."

"I'm sorry," the ewe quavered. "I knew that would probably be the response. And I don't have any visible scars."

"Well then." The shepherd smiled confidently. "That means you're healed, right? It's beautiful what God can do! Let's sing some Scripture songs."

"But you have two witnesses now!" the woman protested. "I saw him attempt to attack a lamb; this ewe testified he attacked her, too. What more do you need?"

I know what we'll do." The shepherd smiled, setting down his Book. He walked over to the wolf, chatted briefly with him, and then led the wolf back over to the woman and the ewe. "Let's talk with him!"

"I can't do it," the ewe whimpered, shrinking back into the flock. "I've been trying to tell you, my life has changed so much since the attack. My anxiety, my depression... You have no idea." She bolted away into the flock and was gone.

The shepherd shrugged. "I guess she was making it up to get attention. They often do that, you know? Sheep love attention."

"This is crazy." The woman glared at the shepherd. Then she turned to the wolf. "I saw you attacking the lamb," she challenged, staring directly into the wolf's eyes. "And the ewe—"

"I'm so sorry if anyone has been hurt," the wolf began. "I've never meant to hurt anyone! I don't know what the ewe is talking about, and I never hurt the lamb, as you saw." He looked up at the woman, tears brimming in his wounded eyes. "This whole situation is tearing my heart out! I love lambs. I've always had a heart for them. Especially after my own childhood as an abused pup—I mean lamb."

"You don't belong in the herd," the woman stated, leveling

her gaze at the wolf. "You need to get out of here and never come back. If you truly care about sheep, stay away from them."

"Now wait a minute there," the shepherd interrupted. "This wolf was just sharing how hurt he has been! He's part of my flock, too. Have you no heart at all?" He leaned over and patted the wolf's shoulder. "Some of us actually care about others! Even if he has hurt a few sheep." The shepherd beamed. "We love him and want to provide a safe place for him to heal."

"What about the real sheep you are called to protect?" the woman asked. "Why do wolves matter so much, and sheep matter so little to you?"

"I don't know what you mean," the shepherd said. "Maybe he hurt some sheep. But we all hurt others sometimes. Are you claiming that you have never hurt anyone in your life?"

"This is an entirely different kind of hurting others! If you read these books," the woman said as she offered her books again, "you will understand that. It takes an almost unimaginable amount of callousness to tear lambs apart, to spend days mingling with the flock, identifying the vulnerable ones, and plotting out how to separate them from the flock and enjoy their juicy flesh. How can you equate that with accidentally bumping into each other while going down the trail too close together?"

"I don't have time or interest in your books," the shepherd responded, putting his arm around the wolf and shoving the woman away. "I've told you, my ministry is about sheep, and I'm not an expert on wolves! The other sheep either haven't seen any problems, or aren't willing to talk about them. So, I'm just going to assume the best, like Jesus would." He led the wolf back to the flock and gave him a hug. "Well, I'm so glad this was all resolved biblically! I hope everyone has a nice day."

He went back to his rock, sat down, and picked up his Bible. "Now, where were we? 'Thus says the Lord God, Behold, I am against the shepherds, and I will require my sheep at their hand...'" He stopped, looking up angrily. "Hey! Why did you lose my place in my Book?"

But the woman was gone, hoping to talk with another shepherd.

2

TRAUMA AND THE PATH FORWARD

Renee just couldn't "get over it." Her pastor was having a hard time understanding. After all, the abuse had happened when she was a child. Now, thirty years later, she kept complaining of nightmares and "flashbacks." She insisted that her inability to control her appetite was a result of her stepfather's assaults—but so was everything else, too, it seemed. Conversations with Rene were often sprinkled with tearful mentions of the diagnoses her counselor had given her: PTSD, attachment disorder, substance abuse due to trauma.

I'm not so sure this counseling is doing much good, her pastor sometimes secretly thought. *Is it really healthy for her to be blaming everything bad in her life on someone else, on something that happened decades ago?* But he never dared to say anything about his doubts regarding the usefulness of her years of counseling. He'd already been warned that this would lead to accusations of "re-traumatization." *This is why I didn't go into the counseling profession,* he would sigh to himself after another talk with a tearful Renee.

Abuse happens. It happens to most of us, to some degree,

at one time or another. It's an inevitable reality of life in a sinful world. But sometimes it seems like victims' responses are more extreme than actual situations. We hear of exhausting years of counseling, diagnoses and medications, ongoing ups and downs. Does it always have to be such a big deal? At some point, shouldn't people just forgive and forget?

The evidence is clear. Abuse, particularly when it occurs in childhood, can cause long- term psychological distress. Our first lesson in healing, whether for ourselves or someone we love, is to understand the effects of abuse trauma. In this chapter, we'll examine some of those effects, and then identify treatments that help survivors break out of destructive cycles. Finally, we'll look at an encouraging phenomenon called post-traumatic growth.

It is inevitable that many of the defenders reading this book are also survivors of abuse themselves. It is our goal to help all of our readers to digest this information and, where possible, apply it to their own experiences. Some of the discussion questions will be directed especially toward helping survivors of abuse to process application of the information in their own progression of healing.

Whether you have suffered abuse yourself, or are an untraumatized defender seeking to help others, the following overview of how abuse damages, and how the damage can be reversed by gospel-oriented responses, is vital.

The Effects of Abuse

For survivors of abuse, assessing the damage is the first step toward healing. Not every person who experiences abuse will develop a diagnosable disorder, but all can benefit from understanding the diagnoses and their markers.

Trauma comes as the result of many experiences, including child abuse, motor vehicle and other accidents, stranger physical assault, intimate partner violence, sex trafficking, natural disasters, torture, war, witnessing homicide or suicide, and even life-threatening medical conditions.

Some who experience trauma will develop a condition called post-traumatic stress disorder, or PTSD. Some will develop other anxiety- or mood-related disorders and symptoms, such as depression, substance abuse disorders, stress disorders, and other disorders that may affect their ability to stay in touch with reality. Many of the effects of trauma lie in the realm of undiagnosable distress that plagues our well-being and relationships in subtle yet significant ways. To better understand the effects of trauma, we'll focus first on PTSD.

To be formally diagnosed with PTSD, a person must directly experience or witness an event that threatens their physical safety. This will produce three symptom clusters called re-experiencing, avoidance, and hyperarousal. [1]

Re-experiencing involves intrusive thoughts, nightmares, flashbacks, extreme triggerability, and intense physical reactions. This re-experiencing can significantly compromise quality of life. A woman who had been sexually assaulted while a certain Christian praise song played in the background couldn't attend church for a long time because the song was very popular and, every time the band sang it, she went "back there." Another woman's rape would be replayed over and over in her nightmares each night, making sleep nearly impossible. Another woman couldn't even hear the name of her abuser without glazing over and replaying the whole event. It is believed that in PTSD, the brain has not properly processed the traumatic memory, and that it is trying to "bring it up" for that purpose.

Avoidance involves avoiding anything that would remind the individual of the trauma, including thoughts, feelings, and memories. Traumatized people in a pattern of avoidance will often have poor recall of events. They may lose interest in pleasurable activities and become detached. Some will change plans frequently as another avoidance pattern. One man who had been severely abused as a child by his uniformed stepfather avoided all contact with law enforcement officials, even driving a much longer route to work to avoid the police station.

Hyperarousal is a state of nervous system activation in which the individual may experience insomnia, irritability, outbursts of anger, difficulty focusing, hyper-alertness, and an easy startle reflex. The arousal circuit of the autonomic nervous system, called the sympathetic response, is "working overtime," and the calming circuit, called the parasympathetic response, seems paralyzed or unable to compensate. A young man's parents noticed a radical shift in his behavior for no apparent reason. Their pleasant, laid-back son became agitated and irritable seemingly overnight. When the parents mentioned this to the son, he admitted he'd been sexually abused by his athletic coach one night in the locker room, and kept it to himself out of fear of being a "tattletale."

PTSD tends to be the result of a discrete event or series of events involving exposure to physical danger or death. However, a newer form of PTSD, called complex PTSD, or C-PTSD, involves more gradual trauma, typically experienced in childhood as the result of abuse and/or living in an unhealthy home environment.

C-PTSD may be defined as a psychological disorder that can develop in response to prolonged, repeated experience of interpersonal trauma where the individual has little or no chance of escape. One woman recalls a filthy home environment with a hypercritical mother who hoarded and a father strung out on cocaine. Although no overt physical or sexual abuse occurred, the chaos at home destroyed the child's sense of security and made healthy relationships nearly impossible.

Perhaps the best-known research on C-PTSD is the Adverse Childhood Experiences (ACE) studies led by Dr. Vincent Felitti. Dr. Felitti worked with Kaiser Permanente's weight loss clinic doing follow-up research on the program dropouts. He discovered that a majority of the dropouts were abused as children. Dr. Felitti and his team interviewed a total of 17,000 dropouts. They learned that abuse and other adverse childhood experiences can provoke a cascade of effects: First, children tended to experience problems with brain development. Then they tended to have social, emotional, and cognitive difficulties. This would make them more likely to develop high-risk behaviors such as drug and alcohol abuse, which lead to disease and disability. People with high ACEs even tended to die earlier! Felitti said, "Our study of the relationship of adverse childhood experiences to adult health status in over 17,000 persons shows addiction to be a readily understandable although largely unconscious attempt to gain relief from well-concealed prior life traumas by using psychoactive materials."[2]

The effects of ACEs are dose-specific—the more "hits," the greater the chance of negative effects.

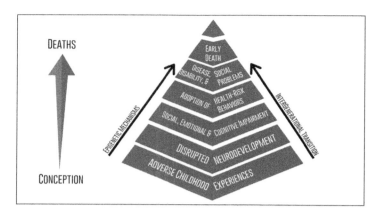

According to Dr. Robert Block, "Adverse childhood experiences are the greatest unaddressed public health threat facing our nation today."[3] More and more attention is being given to adverse childhood experiences, because of their powerful ability to predict other physical and mental conditions.

(To take the ACE test, which is a simple series of 10 questions, see the appendix.)

Helpful Treatments for Trauma

Fortunately, people can recover from the effects of abuse. The endless distress you or your loved one may be feeling right now will not last forever. Trained, trauma-informed counselors can help you regain your sense of peace and security. They may recommend a number of different treatment approaches. Here are some that have been shown to be effective:

Simple disclosure is the first and most often-utilized treatment. Simply sharing the story of trauma with another human being who cares can be a powerful agency of healing. This sharing often occurs in an informal setting with friends or loved ones, or sometimes with a professional counselor, chaplain, or other helper.

Daoud Hari, who translated for journalists during the Darfur crisis in Sudan, saw simple disclosure used with the hordes of people who'd become homeless because of the war. He said, "It helps many people just to have someone listen and write their story down; if their suffering is noted somewhere, by someone, then they can more easily let loose of it because they know where it is."[4]

You can't carry this trauma alone, and you shouldn't have to. "Bear one another's burdens, and so fulfill the law of Christ" (Galatians 6:2). We're only as sick as our secrets. Let someone carry yours, lest they crush you.

Eye movement desensitization and reprocessing (EMDR) was discovered by psychologist Francis Shapiro as she walked in a park. She noticed that thinking about a traumatic event in her life didn't cause as much distress due to the walking. She developed a method of creating a similar effect in counseling offices using right- and left-hand probes, lights, or even gentle tapping on the right and left knee or shoulder. Neuroscientists don't know how this changes the brain, but there are several theories.

One is that EMDR connects the right and left hemispheres of the brain and makes it possible for the negative material in the right to access the positivity of the left hemisphere (The right hemisphere inclines toward pessimism; the left, toward optimism). Another theory says EMDR connects the higher brain with the lower brain, improving its ability to cognitively process challenging material. Whatever the mechanism, the alternating left-right stimulation of the brain seems to put it in a better condition to process trauma. Walking itself can be useful in this way. How often walking with a friend, discussing one's deep troubles, can make the path forward more clear.

Cognitive behavioral therapy (CBT) addresses the distorted thoughts that develop as a result of trauma. Trauma causes a state of chronic arousal of the emotional part of the brain, which can divert energy from the thinking, rational part of the brain (the cerebral cortex, particularly the frontal lobe) and lead to "emotional reasoning," where the person bases their concept of reality on their emotions. Traumatized people often experience the emotions of a dangerous situation after they have returned to a safe one, making those emotions inaccurate. CBT helps correct this imbalance and restore the person's ability to think clearly. Those thoughts in turn change the emotions.

Experiential therapies that involve non-verbal processing of emotions can be helpful in many cases. Animal-assisted therapies such as equine (horse) therapy, as well as art and music therapies can help traumatized individuals process intense emotions. Sensorimotor therapies teach traumatized people how to experience their emotions without becoming overwhelmed.

Relaxation and recounting of events is a slightly more complex form of simple disclosure, utilizing deep breathing, muscle tensing and relaxing, and sometimes prayer, to induce a state of deep relaxation. The goal is to create a new association between the traumatic memory and a state of peace, which can replace the old association of trauma and distress. (For a simple relaxation exercise, see the appendix.)

Biblical counseling (not to be confused with nouthetic counseling) often utilizes a variety of these treatments, and also includes walking a person through applying the gospel directly to their situation. It may involve working through and processing how Jesus suffered every abuse and injustice we suffer, evaluating how our anxiety and depression may result partially from, and exacerbate, sinful responses to trauma, and other approaches. A truly biblical approach will not simply prescribe Bible passages to read or memorize, but will involve a counselor reflecting the caring love of God toward the survivor of abuse through listening and asking thought-provoking questions. Ultimately, biblical counseling will rely on biblical wisdom, searching for applicable insights to heal emotional, relational and spiritual brokenness.

Post-Traumatic Growth

Given the devastating effects of trauma, some question whether any good can come out of it. Post-traumatic growth (PTG) research has made it clear that it can. God promises, "For our light affliction, which is but for a moment, is working for us a far more exceeding and eternal weight of glory" (2 Corinthians 4:17). The affliction doesn't feel light at the time, but in the grand scheme of eternity, it shrinks. And more importantly, it "works" for us by ultimately improving our life, relationships, and character.

However, one of the authors of post-traumatic growth research, Lawrence Calhoun, cautions that "The presence of post-traumatic growth will not necessarily result in an equivalent reduction in distress."[5] The person who experiences PTG may also experience all the unsettling effects of PTSD at the same time. God doesn't always deliver us out of tribulation, but He always grows us in tribulation.

In December of 2018, tour guide Kay Wilson and her friend were attacked by Arab terrorists in a forest near Jerusalem. Kay's friend died, but Kay lived. Though bleeding from 13 stab wounds, with a dislocated shoulder, punctured lungs and diaphragm, and a broken shoulder blade and sternum, Kay crawled to safety.

Kay has since become a living example of PTG, speaking out on recovery, forgiveness, love, and relationships, hoping to dispel the very hatred that led to her near-death. She says, "I believe with an imperfect faith that the question is not 'why' did this happen to me, but rather 'how' can I incorporate this grisly event into the rhythm of my life in a manner that guards me from becoming like those who tried to murder me. I believe with an imperfect faith in a God of justice who has promised that vengeance is His."[6]

Post-traumatic growth says people can actually improve because of trauma. This improvement can take place in five areas:

1. Appreciation of life
2. Relationships with others
3. New possibilities in life
4. Personal strength
5. Spiritual change

In other words, trauma doesn't always bring permanent destruction. It can also deepen people. It can lead them to care more about relationships, and sometimes opens their minds to new possibilities and strengths they didn't know existed. Most significantly, it can lead people closer to their Creator and Redeemer.

Not everyone experiences PTG, but certain traits predict that it will occur. It should be our goal to help provide these for abuse survivors within our community. They are:

1. Social support before and after the trauma
2. Opportunity for emotional disclosure
3. Spirituality
4. Acceptance coping

"Acceptance coping" means eventually and ultimately accepting what happened, rather than repeatedly rehearsing it with regret. We can reflect on the words of Joseph, a man sold into slavery by his brothers, unlawfully imprisoned but then fortuitously promoted to be prime minister of Egypt.

In response to his brothers' remorse at betraying him, he said, "You meant evil against me, but God meant it for good" (Genesis 50:20). The God of the universe is able to harness even the ill will of abusers to accomplish ultimate good. The abusers write a chapter of our story—but in partnership with God, we write the rest of the book. (For help assessing post-traumatic growth, see "Post-traumatic Growth Inventory" in Additional Resources.)

We must never baptize or trivialize the horror of abuse and the trauma that comes from it. But identifying the ways in which God can turn it around for good is an essential part of recovery and healing. After all, isn't this reflective of the larger picture of the battle the world is currently caught in, between the forces of good and evil? Someday, it is God's intention that His people will be more like Him, not just in spite of the traumas inflicted by sin, *but actually because of its one-time existence in the universe.*

So, while evil is always against God's *will,* He is able to use evil to accomplish His greater *purpose* of leading the universe to understand His love better, especially as we contrast it with the evil we have witnessed. Ultimately, the great controversy between God and Satan teaches us that sin itself will eventually immunize the universe against ever breaking God's law of love again. Likewise, trauma can lead survivors to stand against evil and abuse as some of the most motivated defenders of other vulnerable people.

It is to this end that we devote this course. Our prayer and purpose is that the defenders who read this book may help survivors heal physically, mentally, emotionally, socially, and spiritually from the devastating effects of abuse, and eventually to be used by God themselves as defenders of the weak.

It is also our prayer that through processing the information in this course, survivors of abuse may heal and become powerful advocates who understand the process of healing. Woven into each chapter is an exploration of that process.

DISCUSSION QUESTIONS

1. The message we often receive about abuse is that it damages people—and that is true. Is there a complementary, redemptive truth that is just as true?

2. How does the great controversy between Christ and Satan reveal that good can come out of evil and abuse?

3. Often abuse changes the way people see themselves, the world, the future, and even God. What are some of the lies the enemy tells about those things through abuse?

Going deeper: Some questions to ask yourself or someone you are helping

4. Were your results on the ACE test surprising to you? How do your results change the way you view yourself and your life experience?

5. Have you experienced any of the markers of PTSD? If so, which ones?

6. The categories of PTSD symptoms can be thought of in three categories: re-experiencing, avoidance, and hyperarousal. Do you relate to any of them? Which ones?

7. One of the most important "treatments" for trauma is

simple disclosure, meaning telling someone you trust about what you experienced. If you have experienced abuse, have you talked about it with a trusted person? If so, who was it and what led you to trust them?

8. Do you have sufficient social support to help you heal? If not, what are some ways you could find that social support?

9. What was the lowest point in your abuse experience?

10. What was the point at which you felt hope that you could heal and reclaim yourself and your future?

3

FORGIVING WITHOUT ENABLING

O ne lovely evening in Madisonville, Louisiana in 1980, Debbie Morris and her boyfriend Mark Brewster sat on a riverfront sipping milkshakes, looking forward to a relaxing evening. Instead, the evening turned into hell itself. Criminals Robert Lee Willie and Joe Vaccaro kidnapped Mark and Debbie, tortured Mark, and terrorized and repeatedly raped Debbie into the night.

By some unexplainable miracle, Debbie was able to talk her captors into letting her go. But the suffering continued. The couple's relationship deteriorated, and Debbie dropped out of high school because of crippling fears. When law enforcement officials caught the abductors, Debbie had the satisfaction of helping the prosecution in a successful bid for the death penalty for Robert Lee Willie, the subject of the book *Dead Man Walking*. But justice didn't have the healing effect she'd hoped. Ultimately, Debbie chose to forgive Robert Lee Willie, a journey she details in her book *Forgiving the Dead Man Walking*.

In order for victims of abuse to become survivors, forgiveness is crucial. So, when abuse has been investigated and found (or strongly suspected) to have happened, we must assist in helping move victims through the process of healing. A crucial part of healing is embracing forgiveness.

The Justice and Mercy Dance

Justice and mercy weave together to create the fabric of love. Without justice, mercy has no meaning. But without mercy, justice condemns us all. When it comes to the abuse question, we can fall into either extreme—that of ignoring justice or that of holding onto sweet revenge until it turns bitter in our souls.

The first lie the devil told was, "You will not surely die" (Genesis 3:4). Sin is the breaking of righteous relationship with God and others. But Satan said sinning against another would have no effect on the relationship. An unrepentant abuser will likewise argue for a business-as-usual response to abuse: a quick fix, shallow excusing of sin, and instantly reinstated trust. Those who insist upon more may hear, "You're being unkind," "You should forgive and forget," and other put-downs. But abusing another human being should never be trivialized by a flaccid response.

Mercy and justice can be seen as a dance weaving gracefully between two sides. In order to experience true forgiveness, many victims need to experience justice first—or at least seek it. Far from being evil, the pursuit of justice is actually a reflection of the character of God. Indeed, He has commanded not just victims, but all of His followers to "seek justice, rebuke the oppressor; defend the fatherless, plead for the widow" (Isaiah 1:17). He even warned that if His people did not do this work of defending the vulnerable, they would be "devoured by the sword" (Isaiah 1:20). "Finding their anger" and experiencing an appropriate sense of outrage is part of victims' eventual, meaningful forgiveness. Skipping this step constitutes excusing—as opposed to forgiving—sin. Rachael Denhollander expressed this brilliantly in her public statement at the trial of Larry Nassar, the doctor who sexually assaulted her and hundreds of other gymnasts. While her entire testimony is perhaps one of the most eye-opening expositions ever presented on the balance of justice and mercy in dealing with sexual abuse and assault, this excerpt is especially powerful.

In our early hearings, you brought your Bible into the courtroom and you have spoken of praying for forgiveness. And so, it is on that basis that I appeal to you. If you have read the Bible you carry, you know the definition of sacrificial love portrayed is of God himself loving so sacrificially that he gave up everything to pay a penalty for the sin he did not commit. By his grace, I, too, choose to love this way.

You spoke of praying for forgiveness. But Larry, if you have read the Bible you carry, you know forgiveness does not come from doing good things, as if good deeds can erase what you have done. It comes from repentance which requires facing and acknowledging the truth about what you have done in all of its utter depravity and horror, without mitigation, without excuse, without acting as if good deeds can erase what you have seen this courtroom today.

The Bible you carry says it is better for a stone to be thrown around your neck and you thrown into a lake than for you to make even one child stumble--and you have damaged hundreds.

The Bible you speak carries a final judgment where all of

God's wrath and eternal terror is poured out on men like you. Should you ever reach the point of truly facing what you have done, the guilt will be crushing. And that is what makes the gospel of Christ so sweet--because it extends grace and hope and mercy where none should be found. And it will be there for you.

I pray you experience the soul-crushing weight of guilt so you may someday experience true repentance and true forgiveness from God, which you need far more than forgiveness from me—though I extend that to you as well.

Many of the testimonies given by victims of Larry Nassar provide a thought-provoking and sobering window into the effects of sexual abuse on victims. Given before his sentencing, they reveal the power of seeking justice in the process of forgiveness. Too many well-meaning people try to hasten the victim into "forgiving and forgetting." They try to persuade victims that to forgive means trusting the abuser and acting like the abuse did not happen. This is a grave mistake—abusers have proven themselves untrustworthy, often to such an extent that they have permanently forfeited the right to be trusted. Furthermore, to "forget" in this context often means "pretend the abuse did not happen." Such "forgetting" is itself a denial of the need to forgive. Extending trust to a person who has demonstrated a pattern of exploiting trust may be exactly the opposite of a loving response—it dangles temptation before the abuser once again.

True forgiveness, however, is best for everyone, including the victims themselves. Lewis Smedes wrote, "To forgive is to set a prisoner free and discover the prisoner was you." In the long term, the forgiver must be able to blend their need with justice with their need to extend mercy, based on the fact that they themselves have been forgiven much by God. The parable of the unforgiving servant is a wonderful study on this topic.

Sin and Debt

The Matthew 18 parable of the unforgiving servant presents sin as a debt to be either compensated or released. In the parable, a king confronts his servant about the servant's debt of millions of dollars. When the king threatens to put the servant and his family in prison, the guilty man pleads, "Have patience with me, and I will pay thee all." The king freely forgives the man, who then ungratefully refuses to forgive his own debtor who owed a far smaller sum. When the servant throws his friend into debtor's prison, the king hears the news and "delivers him to the tormentors" (Matthew 18:34). Jesus ended this parable with the warning that the same would happen to those who didn't forgive.

Sin is a debt the sinner owes to God and to human beings they have harmed. Perpetrators of abuse owe their victims for the suffering they have caused them. Victims can seek to collect on the debt, or they can release the perpetrator to the justice of God. In so doing, victims take those who have harmed them off the "hook" of their own justice, and place them on God's "hook," knowing that the God who reads hearts, and who died for sinners, will balance justice and mercy perfectly in each case.

In the Lord's Prayer, Jesus said, "Forgive us our debts *as* we forgive our debtors" (Matthew 6:12). Forgiveness simultaneously flows into our hearts from God and out from us to others. Forgiveness may be seen as a door we open in our souls, out of which God's grace flows. Should we close that door, we close the only avenue through which God's grace can flow back into our own souls. Effectively, this bars the way for our own forgiveness.

Forgiveness Supplied and Forgiveness Applied

Can we forgive someone who isn't sorry? In abuse situations, the perpetrator often denies, excuses, or dismisses their crimes. Or what if they apologize, but only half-heartedly and without restitution? What can help us navigate through these tough questions is that forgiveness has two basic phases: forgiveness supplied and forgiveness applied.

Forgiveness supplied is the forgiveness we hold in our hearts for the unrepentant person. Jesus said, "Whenever you stand praying, if you have anything against anyone, forgive him, that your Father in heaven may also forgive your trespasses" (Mark 11:25).

Forgiveness applied is forgiveness bestowed upon someone who is truly, deeply repentant. Jesus said, "If your brother sins against you, rebuke him; and if he repents, forgive him" (Luke 17:3). Notice that forgiveness is "if" he repents. The forgiveness we hold in store for our abusers can only be applied by God personally *if* they truly repent. In other words, when victims forgive, they release themselves from bondage to bitterness. They entrust the abuser to the justice of God, who reads hearts and will only wipe away the guilt if the abuser truly repents.

Notice also that rebuke of the brother precedes his repentance. Many fallen people lack a clear idea of the harm they've caused and need a sharp, clear, reminder. "Rebuke" is from the Greek *epitiamao,* and can mean a formal process of discipline.

One definition of *epitiamao* is "showing honor to." By endorsing formal discipline for sexual abuse, we're telling a person, "You're better than this."

Ty Gibson has said, "Forgiveness is the decision to cease holding a person's offenses against them to their hurt."[1] Our desire to encourage appropriate consequences stems not from vengeance, but from wanting to help the perpetrator and everyone else involved. Victims may release abusers from their debt, but they should not release them from redemptive consequences. As the Old Testament abundantly demonstrates, painful consequences for sin are often the best, or even only, way to bring a persistent sinner to true repentance. This is, admittedly, a hard balance to strike, but a vital one.

The Steps

We can see forgiveness as a series of steps. But we must take these steps over and over again. Forgiveness isn't an event, but rather, a lifestyle.

1. Define Forgiveness

To define forgiveness means to identify what it is, but also what is it not. Forgiveness is *not* several things we often mistake it for:

Trusting—Forgiveness can be one-sided, but trust demands the willing, conscious participation of two parties. Forgiveness is free, but trust is earned. If someone has abused, we may forgive them freely, but still hold them accountable for what they did, and only trust again if they show signs of deep repentance. This includes a humble acknowledgement that trust has been broken and that they have no right to demand that others trust them.

Reconciliation—Similarly, reconciliation requires a rebuilding process that may or may not be appropriate in cases of abuse. When abuse has occurred, that relationship has been permanently altered. Attempts to make things go back to the way they were often spring from a denial of those changes and a desire to evade consequences.

Excusing—Forgiveness has justice built right into it. When we forgive someone, we don't say, "No big deal, it's okay." Instead, we say, "It *is* a big deal, but I forgive you."

Approving—Similarly, when we forgive, we're showing a clear disdain for what was done and acknowledging that while in one sense we have a right to exact revenge, we have released that right.

Forgetting—The abuse has become part of our personal narrative and can't be forgotten without compromising our story. Demanding that victims forget is often the fruit of the perpetrator's shallow repentance and desire to hide from the truth. A healthy survivor will retain the right to their own testimony, while avoiding dwelling on the abuse in a way that retraumatizes them.

Feeling—We often want a choice to forgive to be attended by tender, warm feelings. That sometimes happens. But feelings don't always go the direction we want them to go. If we have a long-standing pattern of resentment toward someone and have chosen to release that resentment, it will usually take time for new synaptic pathways to form. Feeling forgiving is particularly difficult if the one who harmed us manifests the same hurtful traits that caused the injury in the first place. We shouldn't over-identify with our emotions, as they do not define us and must not control us.

Forgiveness does not mean trusting, reconciling, excusing,

approving, forgetting, or feeling. It is a choice to let go of bitterness and resentment and to release our abusers from the debt incurred through sin. This can't be done without careful consideration and divine help--but all things are possible with God.

2. Establish Distance

Forgiving is a process, and the brain usually can't process much in the heat of an abusive situation. This is why separation and boundaries are so essential to our ability to forgive. Where physical separation is impossible, emotional separation may be the only option.

3. Survey the Damage

In order to forgive, a person must know not just *who* but *what* they are forgiving. It may help to identify a few of the various categories of damage, which we will explore in more detail later:

- Harm to children
- Cultural damage
- Emotional wounds
- Financial cost
- Intellectual harm
- Harm to property/pets
- Physical harm
- Psychological wounds
- Sexual wounds
- Social destruction
- Spiritual harm
- Verbal wounds

Ask yourself, "Did (the person) cause (the category—physical, sexual, spiritual, etc.) damage? What was it? Is the damage permanent? Were others I love damaged too?" You may feel guilty counting up the sins of another against you, but remember the goal is to thoroughly forgive the person. A gloss-over of wrong done will leave roots of resentment in the soil of the heart. Over-blame is certainly a problem, but some of us under-blame others and over-blame ourselves for things we could not control. This step helps us identify the truth in objective terms.

4. Count the Cost

Remember that forgiveness is a choice to let go of bitter-ness and resentment, and from our side, to release the abuser from the debt incurred through sin. Forgiveness thus removes our "right" to seek revenge; instead, it puts us in a place to seek to do right because it is right. We do right, not because we want to cause pain or "get even," but in order to do what is best for the abuser and others (including ourselves) who need justice or protection. In order to make a conscious choice, we must identify the pros and cons of that choice.

A victim may need to take a sheet of paper and write "for-give" and "don't forgive" at the top. Beneath each of those words, they can put "pros" and "cons" columns, and write down everything they can think of under those columns. Doing the exercise on paper will make it more effective. Exam-ining these lists together can help defenders be equipped to assist victims in making decisions based on the results.

5. Remain Self-Aware

The victim's sins may be smaller and less significant than the abuser's, but all of us have the potential of being the worst of sinners, and all of us need forgiveness. For a person with a history of unhealthy self-blame, this may feel like a lapse back into dysfunctional self-blame, but remember, you're being guided by the *facts*. Jesus made it clear in his parable of the two debtors (Luke 7) that Simon bore ten times the guilt for abusing Mary. But He said Mary's sins were "many" (vs. 47). It's entirely possible to be both a sinner and a victim of others' sins at the same time.

Taking appropriate account of our own sins has a psychological benefit. An "external locus of control" in which people feels life "happens" to them, and that they are simply victims of circumstances, predicts anxiety, mood issues, addiction, and other harmful patterns. An "internal locus of control" brings about the opposite—a sense of self-efficacy and stability. Taking a fearless moral inventory of ourselves can thus actually make us less vulnerable to abuse.

It's not your fault someone abused you. What you do in response *is* your responsibility.

6. Repeat Often

Forgiveness is not a singular event; it's a lifestyle. We may have to forgive our abusers again and again. Should we lapse back into bitterness, resentment, and self-pity, we can just get up, brush ourselves off, and try again. A pattern repeated over and over will eventually "stick" and become easier. Letting go of bitterness and resentment requires effort, but the effort will pay off in the end.

God Gives Wisdom

In many cases of abuse, consequences for the wrong will be the right choice. Consequences make a statement of the seriousness of the crime committed. They help the community feel safer; they even help the perpetrator wake up to the enormity of the crime. For instance, someone who perpetrates sexual assault on a child should go to jail, no matter how repentant they are (or claim to be). This is a matter of safety and basic justice. Agreeing and even assisting in bringing these consequences doesn't mean that the victim is not forgiving the perpetrator. The victim may release the perpetrator from the spiritual debt of sin, and still approve of temporal consequences.

Much of discerning whether or not someone has forgiven has to do with spirit and motive, which are difficult for onlookers to judge. Does the victim desire consequences for perpetrators of abuse out of resentment, bitterness, and hatred? Or out of love for all concerned? The Green River Killer raped and murdered 48 women. During the victim disclosure period of his trial, one victim's father, Robert Rule, publicly forgave him. Many had preceded him with hateful speeches, but Mr. Rule chose forgiveness. Nothing prepared the killer, Gary Ridgeway, for this. Though he had thus far shown no remorse, at the offer of Mr. Rule's forgiveness, the rapist and murderer wept in the courtroom. Shortly after this, he received the death penalty. Mr. Rule didn't protest that, but he did release Ridgeway from the spiritual debt of the infinite loss of his daughter.

Forgiving an abuser without enabling requires a mature understanding of God's justice and mercy, and how they intersect. This can be a messy, conflicted process. Those struggling with it should allow themselves time to work through its complexities, trusting that He will guide and help them. "If any of you lacks wisdom, let him ask of God, who gives to all liberally and without reproach, and it will be given to him" (James 1:5).

DISCUSSION QUESTIONS

1. What do abusers want to deny about how sin affects relationships, and why?

2. What does it mean to take abusers off our "hook" and put them on God's "hook"? How is this related to trusting in God's ability to judge hearts and balance justice and mercy perfectly for this person?

3. "Rebuke" can mean "show honor to." How does it show honor to rebuke someone who has done wrong?

4. What aspects of establishing distance between a victim and an abuser make it possible to forgive?

5. How does remaining aware of our own sinfulness keep us from descending into bitterness and resentment?

6. Give your own definition of forgiveness.

7. Share a situation in which you forgave but also embraced the need for consequences.

8. Share a time when you overlooked or excused sin out of convenience, and realized it was a bad idea.

Going deeper: Some questions to ask yourself or someone you are helping

9. Of all the things that forgiveness is *not,* which ones have you tended to believe the most? Illustrate one with a personal experience.

10. When an abuser reaps consequences for abuse, victims may feel guilty, as if they're being unchristian. What has helped you personally come to terms with appropriate consequences?

4

VICTIM, SURVIVOR, THRIVER, DEFENDER

This chapter pulls together the two primary goals of this book: 1) to equip defenders to help survivors heal, and 2) to equip victims themselves to heal. Often these two goals are intertwined, especially since many of the most passionate and able defenders are themselves survivors of abuse. We heal to serve—and in serving, we heal. If we could help every victim of abuse to move through the process of becoming a survivor, thriver, and then a defender of other victims, we would raise up such an army of defenders that the enemy wouldn't stand a chance against us.

Let's restate that with more faith. *As* we help every victim of abuse to move through the process of being a survivor, thriver, and defender of other victims, we *will* raise up such an army of defenders that the enemy won't stand a chance against us. Now, let's dig in and see how it's done.

The Nature of Love

An understanding of the love of God drives and energizes

the healing process. "God is love. His nature, His law, is love. It ever has been; it ever will be."[1] This love holds infinite regenerative power for the body, soul, and spirit of God's sin-damaged children. "Only by love is love awakened."[2] Through the revelation of the gospel and the love of God contained in it, the little flowers of hope start to grow again in hearts that have been damaged by the enemy's blight.

Love cannot exist apart from freedom. If a suitor holds a gun to his lady's head, she may comply with his wishes, but she will never love him with her heart. In attempting to force her, he has made love impossible. God designed the emotional processes of love—from neurons, to neurotransmitters, to brain circuits, to psychological responses, to attachment behaviors—to be enlivened through the free exercise of the will. Love is a choice, or it doesn't exist at all; true love always respects the agency and choices of the other.

Understanding this freedom-love connection protects us from being trapped in false intimacy based on control. Abuse always entails dominance of the will of the more vulnerable person. This manifests the spirit of the enemy of God, the spirit that seeks the highest place. Lucifer said, "I will ascend above the heights of the clouds; I will be like the Most High" (Isaiah 14:14). He sought to ascend, even to the point of attempting to steal the throne of God Himself. Jesus came as a Lamb to sacrifice Himself on a lonely Cross. The corrupt creature tried to be God, while God Himself took the corruption of the creature. The enemy loves power. God lives for the power of love.

In seeking the lowest place, we lift others higher. Think of braiding three strands. Each time a new strand weaves its way down into the center of the braid, it pushes up the other two.

"A threefold cord is not quickly broken" (Ecclesiastes 4:12) because each cord ministers to and lifts up the others. Our relationships become indestructible when we exercise this one principle.

Love in the Family

Understanding this principle of love informs healthy parenting and families. God ordained that parents and other caregivers reflect his unconditional love to the young ones in the family system. When those in power misrepresent God, they warp the child's sense of worth and lovability. This reflects back on the child's God-concept and leads them to believe God is unloving.

Abuse mars our picture of God and ourselves, thus striking at the heart of our ability to obey God's law. How can we respond in love to a God who appears unloving and untrustworthy? How can we love our neighbors as ourselves? The fact that abuse so deeply affects our spiritual life is good news--it means that the gospel can and will heal these wounds, when properly applied.

Individuals who have survived abuse—particularly child abuse—have been disadvantaged emotionally, morally, relationally, and spiritually. The human heart is like a sponge. We were created to absorb God's love, and nothing else can satisfy us. But a heart that has been damaged by abuse becomes encased in lies, making it difficult to soak up divine love. Imagine a sponge in a Ziploc bag, immersed in water. It can be left in the water for hours, but it remains dry because it is encased in plastic. Through abuse, the enemy encases our hearts in lies. We are then sorely tempted to doubt God's love and power. Abused people ask, "If God loves me and could deliver me, why didn't He? Either He isn't strong enough, or He isn't loving enough, to protect me."

The Word of God teaches that God *is* love and *wants* to end suffering, and that He *is* almighty and *able* to end suffering. But God is engaging in a thorough process of ending suffering by ending the sin that caused the suffering in the first place. In order to end sin, God must work with the free wills of the creatures that can choose either His service or the service of sin.

This persuasion process takes longer than we would like! In fact, this struggle to end sin is sometimes called "the cosmic conflict" because it focuses on the big-picture dynamics between God, Lucifer, humanity, and all of human history. Because of our shortsightedness, we want God to take away the suffering now, not realizing that He's doing all He can now to end it for once and for all. If we doubt God's love during this waiting time, we must look at the Cross and remember God has shown that there is nothing He wouldn't give for the good of His children.

The story of God's struggle to end sin teaches us that pain is not the real enemy—sin is the enemy. God can even *use* pain to help sinners learn to hate and overcome the sin that brought suffering in the first place. Specifically, the horrible pain we suffer because of abuse isn't the worst part of the abuse situation. The worst thing is the abuse itself--sin, which rips the hearts of God's people away from His great heart of love. God wants to end the pain of abuse once and for all. In order to do that, He must take the abusiveness out of the hearts of His children, and give them hearts that love and worship Him.

Some won't allow that. Some will cling to their sin and refuse God's gift of repentance (See 2 Timothy 2:24-26; Acts 5:31). The Bible is clear that unrepentant abusive people will be destroyed in the end.

. . .

The Destruction of Evil People

"Because they do not regard the works of the Lord, nor the operation of His hands, He shall destroy them and not build them up" (Psalm 28:5).

"But the transgressors shall be destroyed together; the future of the wicked shall be cut off" (Psalm 37:38).

"He has brought on them their own iniquity, and shall cut them off in their own wickedness. The Lord our God shall cut them off" (Psalm 94:23).

"The house of the wicked will be overthrown, but the tent of the upright will flourish" (Proverbs 14:11).

"Woe to them, for they have fled from Me! Destruction to them, because they have transgressed against Me! Though I redeemed them, yet they have spoken lies against Me" (Hosea 7:13).

"These shall be punished with everlasting destruction from the presence of the Lord and from the glory of His power" (2 Thessalonians 1:9).

"But these, like natural brute beasts made to be caught and destroyed, speak evil of the things they do not understand, and will utterly perish in their own corruption" (2 Peter 2:12).

"But the heavens and the earth which are now preserved by the same word, are reserved for fire until the day of judgment and perdition of ungodly men" (2 Peter 3:7).

"If anyone worships the beast and his image, and receives his mark on his forehead or on his hand, he himself shall also drink of the wine of the wrath of God" (Revelation 14:9-10).

The Church

When we receive deep wounds in relationships, we sometimes think that removing ourselves from all relationships will help us heal. But it doesn't work that way. Tim Clinton says, "We were wounded in relationships, and we are healed in them, too. We won't make much progress on our own."[3] This is where the church can become a mighty instrument in God's hands to heal the broken. It's almost as if a "re-parenting" takes place when we are adopted into the family of God.

Some of us have been wounded in church. This can make it hard to ever trust the church again. But God would like us to know that if church leaders and members failed to protect us from abuse, they did so in disobedience of His clear instructions to "remove the wicked man from amongst yourselves" (1 Corinthians 5:13). In other words, when abuse happens in church, it's because of human failure, not God's failure. In an earthly family, an abusive father has *failed* at being a true father. In the family of God, abusive and complicit leaders are *failing* to be true servant leaders. If the church functioned as the loving family God intended, the vulnerable members of the flock would be protected by the stronger members. We're told to "Deliver the poor and needy; free them from the hand of the wicked" (Psalm 82:4). If all followed this command, there would be no abuse in the family of God.

It may be that when you needed such protective leaders, they were not there. The best way for you to overcome those feelings of powerlessness is to become a protector yourself. This is why this book was written—to help people heal, and to equip people to help in healing others. Often those who were once wounded themselves become the most compassionate and courageous in helping others heal.

Abuse can make the climb of life steeper. Imagine a person walking up a slight hill. That person gets a little winded, but the climb is comfortable. Now imagine someone clambering up a mountain. They struggle for breath, sweat, and get sore muscles. They may have to take more rests to make the climb. But lo and behold, at the end of the climb, their muscles are stronger than they would have been with a gentler slope—a consolation prize for the struggling climber.

For a person who grew up in an abusive environment, the faith struggle requires a steeper climb than for those who have not suffered abuse. Such it is for the soul who has suffered abuse. Believing in God can be tougher than it would have been otherwise, but faith muscles build in the process of choosing to believe that God is who He says He is, not who we feel He is, or who life circumstances have seemed to indicate He is.

Defenders

On a cosmic scale, those who have been abused by Satan, but who choose faith in God's love anyway, become the most powerful witnesses of the love of God. Likewise, because of the hard work they must do to thrive, survivors of abuse have the potential for becoming some of the most effective advocates, educators, and defenders.

Consider the ancient art of kintsugi. Kintsugi is the Japanese art called "golden joinery," which takes broken pieces and joins them together with resin or lacquer, then another layer of resin mixed with real gold, making the pottery more beautiful because of its repairs. God doesn't cause abuse, but He does a masterful job of piecing us back together with the gold of faith tried in the fire, yielding a work of art that takes away the breath of the entire universe.

Empathy

The suffering involved in abuse can form the basis of the gift of empathy for others who have suffered. God makes us beautiful and effective by helping our empathy flourish. Human beings are endowed with wonderful units called mirror neurons. Scientists discovered them while testing primates. One monkey ate a banana while the other watched, and the scientists saw the other monkey's brain light up *as if he was eating the banana*. If a monkey's brain can experience empathy, how much more can a human brain experience?

Empathy includes many features:

- Showing concern and care for others
- Paying attention to the needs of others
- Listening to others rather than merely talking at them
- Getting to know someone rather than judging them

- Asking someone how they're feeling if you sense something wrong
- Learning about people from different backgrounds and cultures

Empathy calls us to experience the joy and pain of others selflessly. (To learn empathic listening, see "Listening Well" in the Additional Resources.) "Be happy with those who are happy and weep with those who weep" (Romans 12:15, NLT). "When others are happy, be happy with them, and when they are sad, be sad" (Romans 12:15, CEV). Without empathy, we cannot feel others' love for us, nor experience and internalize the impact of the Cross. Without empathy, we nullify the power of the gospel to transform our hearts. With empathy, we can feel the pain of others, understand the love of God, and embrace the power of the gospel to transform us and others.

Pain is God's most effective empathy-teaching tool. At the same time, it teaches us hatred of sin. Abuse, which never should have existed, can be redeemed by God. The pain we experience because of abuse doesn't have to destroy us at all. It can actually form the basis of character development, growth in love, increased empathy, and a better understanding of the gospel, ultimately fitting us to become effective defenders of the weak.

The worst thing that has ever happened is the crucifixion, where humanity murdered God. The best thing that has ever happened is the Cross, where God saved humanity. The worst and the best are contained in the same event. God recycled the abuse of the crucifixion into the salvation of the Cross. He will recycle our abuse too.

DISCUSSION QUESTIONS

1. How do control, manipulation, and force destroy love?

2. Share a time in your life when someone took the lowest place to lift you up.

3. How does abuse alter a victim's perception of God?

4. Does abuse make it impossible for victims to know God? Or does it just make it more difficult?

5. What does the Bible teach regarding God's power, His love, and how they intersect in the cosmic conflict?

6. Suffering is indeed a bad thing. But what is the greatest enemy of all, and why?

7. What is God doing to end suffering in the universe?

8. What are some of the benefits that come from survivors of abuse having to work extra hard to believe in a loving God?

9. What is empathy and how does it help us develop as defenders?

10. What is the worst thing that has ever happened to you? Are you willing to give it to Jesus so He can recycle it to become something that equips you to be a defender?

5

IDENTIFYING PERPETRATORS

"*Give justice to the poor and the orphan; uphold the rights of the oppressed and the destitute.*" (*Psalm* 82:3, *NLT*)

Our Biblical Mandate

When we identify perpetrators—when we protect the vulnerable—we fulfill a fundamental biblical mandate. Micah 6:8 says God requires us:

to do justice,

to love mercy, and

to walk humbly.

Examine the verbs in those three commands. Which are we supposed to do, and which are we supposed to love? Often when it comes to situations of abuse, the church *loves* justice (or at least claims to), but *does* mercy. But God's command is to *do* justice, even while *loving* mercy. The requirement here is to protect the vulnerable in our families, churches, and workplaces. We are to love mercy, but we need to keep our communities as safe as possible by *doing* justice.

We cannot make our communities safe for the vulnerable while we are making them hospitable and welcoming for unsafe people. But it takes less effort to offer refuge for unsafe people. All the unsafe person asks is that the people of God look the other way. Far too often, the church has complied--we have worked so hard to make the sheepfold safe for the wolves that we have ignored the sheep bleeding out at our feet. All the abuser asks is for us to smile, show "grace," and maintain the status quo. But God asks more. The vulnerable ones, the victims, need more. Loyal followers of God must be willing to get down in the mess. We must put effort into figuring out the truth, and standing up for it. We must look past our biases. That's hard, and it takes time. We're busy, it's messy and ugly, and often there's a high cost to obeying the biblical commands.

Disturbing Facts You Need to Know

It is a mistake to assume that abusers only target children. They may also target teens or adults for abuse, and they usually groom families or even entire communities in order to get access to their victims. This can be considered its own form of abuse, for it is certainly traumatizing for parents, pastors, or others to realize that they have overlooked or even unwittingly assisted in giving predators opportunities to abuse. But for the sake of the discussion here, we are primarily referring to the abuse of the actual victims targeted. Abusers may be male or female, mature or youthful. We recognize that abuse victims may also be male or female, regardless of the gender of the abuser.

While the following disturbing facts refer largely to children, it is important to keep in mind that any community or congregation has vulnerable people of all ages. While outlined predominantly in the context of minor victims, signs of testing, grooming, and abusing will often transfer to adult-on-adult abuse situations as well.

"Wherever sexual abuse of children occurs, there are unwitting parents or caregivers witnessing the performance that precedes the crime."[1] In her chilling book *Predators*, Anna Salter reveals that one in three girls and one in six boys will have sexual contact with an adult. She also points out that:

- Only five out of every 1,000 rapists go to jail[2]
- The most common age at which sexual abuse begins is three years old
- More than two-thirds of sexual assault victims are juveniles
- One in seven victims of sexual assault is under the age of six[3]
- Most sexual abuse is committed by heterosexual males, not homosexuals[4]
- The average sexual predator has 50 to 150 victims before their first arrest, and many more after[5]
- Rarely does an initial arrest result in prosecution
- The FBI estimates that on average, there is one sex offender per square mile in the United States[6]

Some child sex offenders are pedophiles (people who have a sexual preference for children), but the majority are not.[7] This is a crucial distinction. Often, when someone says a child is being abused, people respond "That's impossible! Joe is a pedophile?" or "How dare you say Sam is a pedophile!"

In reality, only a small percentage of those who sexually

abuse children actually have a sexual preference for children. Child sexual abuse is about control and dominance, not primarily about sexual preference. Child abusers have significant crossover rates, often committing other types of sexual abuse. In the context of spiritual realities, this is not shocking. At the point where one's conscience has sufficiently deteriorated to make harming a child appealing, what holds the perpetrator back from other types of violence and harm?

Three Types of Child Abusers

Sexual offenders against children come in three types:

1) pedophile — a person whose sexual preference is prepubescent children.

2) child predator — a person who takes time and intentionally schemes to create opportunities to offend against children.

3) child molester — a person who sexually abuses a child for whatever reason, such as impulse, convenience, experimentation, etc.

Both child molesters and child predators may have a heterosexual preference for adults, but they molest children of any gender simply because they can, or because they like the thrill of getting away with it. Taking it from a different angle, someone who has sexually molested a child is a child molester —regardless of whether or not they are a calculated child predator or a pedophile with a distinct sexual preference for children. Someone who has molested a child is not automatically a pedophile or a child predator. This is important to understand because each type of abuser may act in very different ways, but all of them harm children.

.   .   .

"Crimes against women and children in the Christian community nearly always depend on the long con. This is an elaborate con which is carried out over time, involving multiple layers of persuasion and credible deceit, not only toward those who are selected as marks, but also toward the people they are likely to trust or go to for counsel and help. A long con in a Christian community may include church membership, marriage, credible testimonies, and no end of touching statements, pietistic looks, and impressive ethical stances."

— Valerie Jacobsen, Advocate & Survivor

If abusers have nefarious intentions, they will absolutely be cultivating positive, perhaps even preferential, relationships with anyone who could eventually stand in the way of them continuing their abuse. An abuser depends on his relationships with those around who will adamantly deny that he is capable of causing harm. He needs friends who will be quick to cry out, "Oh my goodness. He would never do such a thing!" Ted Bundy volunteered to answer calls to a rape hotline. We mustn't overestimate our ability to see past a good appearance.

Two Types of Sexual Predators

There are two types of predator: the power predator and the persuasion predator.

A power predator assaults suddenly, violently. This is the rape in a dark alley. This predator assaults, causes harm, and runs away. There is no ongoing relationship. They strike only when they feel certain they will succeed.

The power predator is the type you think of when you

teach your kids about "Stranger Danger." In reality, more than 90% of assaults on children are by someone they trust and know. Stranger Danger is a tiny fraction of those causing harm against children. Teaching children to watch for strangers may be helpful, but it overlooks the greatest potential danger—tricky people they already trust.

Persuasion predators are far more common. These intentionally choose vulnerable victims. They test boundaries, cultivate trusting relationships, and develop positive reputations with the community—parents, teachers, pastors, leaders, onlookers. They're everyone's favorite.

They test low-risk strategies and gradually escalate. What will this parent let me get away with? What will that observer defend me for? Can I create an atmosphere of misunderstanding, and then have everyone believe me when I say it was a misunderstanding?

The persuasion predator deftly separates the target from the flock, often without even appearing to cause isolation, and spends an extraordinary amount of time cultivating and depending on misplaced trust.

The Narcissistic Spectrum

One easy way to remember perpetrator traits is with the acronym CHIN:

C - Charisma

H - Hero complex

I - Insularity

N - Narcissism

These traits are commonly seen among perpetrators, whether they are extroverted or introverted, jovial or quiet.

Charisma and charm often result in being able to get people to do things their way. A hero complex (or its inverse, the martyr complex) creates a sense of alliance among those around them. Insularity feeds on those alliances, almost like a personality cult. Somehow, their needs tend to come first (even if they make a great show of serving others), and they are simply able to get away with things.

If we look through the lens of the gospel, we are all narcissistic, to some extent. Why? Because sin gives us a bent toward selfishness. Now, secular psychologists may present narcissism as an incurable disease. But narcissism, at its core, is simply extreme vanity, selfishness, and self-absorption.

When we look at narcissism through the gospel lens, we see Christ at one end of the spectrum and Lucifer at the other. Christ is all-giving; Satan is all-taking. Satan crushes everyone in order to exalt himself; Jesus empties Himself, taking the form of a servant. Each of us falls somewhere on that spectrum of sinful self-focus. The more we lean toward Lucifer's all-taking end of the spectrum: the more narcissistic we have chosen to become, the more we are reflecting the character of Lucifer instead of God, the more we are searing our conscience on a day-by-day basis, the more we choose to reject Christ's attitude of empathy and surrender.

Misplaced Trust

Anna Salter says, "Sex offenders only very rarely sneak into a house in the middle of the night. More often, they come through the front door in the day, as friends and neighbors, as Boy Scout leaders, priests, principals, teachers, doctors, and coaches. They are invited into our homes time after time, and we give them permission to take our children on the overnight camping trip, the basketball game, or down to the Salvation Army post for youth activities."[8]

We hand our children off because of misplaced trust. "We think sex offenders must be monsters—and we surely would recognize a monster, wouldn't we?"[9] And so, we give permission because we do not recognize the predator's capability for deceit.

Many abuse experts talk about grooming, but grooming isn't everything. Jimmy Hinton, son of a pedophile and an expert in recognizing techniques of abusers, says that for abusers, "it's about testing people, reading them, feeling them out, and knowing which techniques work best for each individual. Once a deceiver knows how this all works, they don't need to slowly groom someone along. They simply test each of us, then use whatever techniques are best suited for us."[10]

Things you can watch for include but are not limited to:

- Prolonged grooming at times, but not always
- Initially innocent on the surface
- Flattering and making the target feel appreciated or special
- Small boundary violations that precede larger ones
- Alone time where the predator creates ways to connect with the target away from those who can intervene
- Develop a sense of need and reliance in the target on what they receive from the predator

"Abusers exploit our perception of vulnerabilities to create more opportunity to abuse. For example, one of the most common and ineffective policies is where churches keep known child molesters from entering a children's wing of the church but still allow them to be elsewhere in close proximity to children (albeit supervised). This policy assumes that 'keeping an eye on' an abuser is enough to hold them accountable and keep them from abusing more victims."[11]

It is not enough.

This is why Paul warns Timothy: ". . . evil people and impostors will go from bad to worse, deceiving and being deceived" (2 Timothy 3:13, NIV). Paul rightly extends no invitation into the church for abusers. He does not tell Timothy to have an open door policy for all in the Ephesian Church. Instead, Paul warns Timothy that they are "having the appearance of godliness, but denying its power. Avoid such people" (2 Timothy 3:5, ESV).

It's often difficult to see things that happen right in front of us, and one of the scariest things to tell parents is that you simply cannot completely protect your children from all possible opportunities for abuse.

What You Can Do

Something abusive will happen to someone you love. No matter how vigilant we are, in a world of sin, abuse and assault keep happening. What *can* we do to protect our children and the vulnerable people within our circles of influence, even now?

It is crucial that we realize two things: first, *how we respond* as those responsible for these children and vulnerable people may largely mitigate, or even neutralize, the damage to victims of the abuse. Will we listen? Will we discern and believe? Perhaps even more importantly, how can we prepare these vulnerable people—our children and others—so that the abuse may be prevented (by recognizing grooming, staying in safe places, telling adults about suspicious behaviors, listening to their instincts, etc.) or stopped (by yelling for help, fighting back, etc.)?

Often we can teach our children, and the other vulnerable people within our circle of influence, to look for signs. We can teach them to be wise. But first, we must be wise ourselves.

"Despite the fact that decades of research have demonstrated that people cannot reliably tell who is lying and who isn't, most people believe they can."[12] When a pastor meets with a sexual predator, confident he will be able to discern whether the abuser is lying, where does that lead? While we have given some broad guidelines here, even a counselor or therapist with years of training and experience cannot always tell when someone is deceiving them. "Despite the psychopath's lack of conscience and lack of empathy for others, he is inevitably better at fooling people than any other type of offender."[13]

While it is crucial to remember that we cannot reliably tell when a liar is lying, it is nevertheless important to avoid ignoring the Holy Spirit speaking through our intuition. Our gut instincts may be limited, but that doesn't mean they should be ignored. If your instincts are giving you warning signals, give yourself permission to take heed, and teach your children to do the same.

So what does this look like in practical terms?

- Monitor children closely
- Talk frequently about abuse issues with children

- Model an environment of believing victims who report
- Role-play with kids about safe touch and being quick to tell
- Teach them to yell "NO!" when someone acts inappropriately
- Read books together
- Respect children's boundaries
- Finally, we must assume reporters are telling the truth, even while we work to assess evidence Research repeatedly indicates that about 95% of the time, the reporters are telling the truth. "Seek justice, correct oppression, bring justice to the fatherless, and plead the widow's cause" (Isaiah 1:17, ESV)

DISCUSSION QUESTIONS

1. What message does it send to wounded sheep when the shepherds primarily protect the reputation and wellbeing of the wolves?

2. Share your reaction to the facts about sexual abuse and predators. Which stood out to you most?

3. What does the differentiation between the three types of child abusers mean to you? How does it impact your perception of those who hurt children?

4. Do you consider yourself to be a discerning person? How does it feel to know that you likely can't tell if an abuser is lying to you?

5. What does your body do when you feel that something is wrong? Do you feel it in your stomach? Your heart? Your throat? Somewhere else?

6. Do you usually listen and act on that feeling when your body tells you things are not okay?

7. Why is it not safe to simply chaperone offenders and keep them away from the children's wing?

8. Does your church or organization do thorough back-

ground checks on all leaders and volunteers, and even on those who do not work directly with children?

9. Why do you think that background checks might not be enough to protect the vulnerable?

10. What can you personally do to protect the vulnerable, since it is proven (particularly when we have emotional ties to the abuser) that we cannot reliably tell when someone is deceiving us?

6

DEFENDERS AS HEALERS

"*Y*ou have been a stronghold to the poor, a stronghold to the needy in his distress, a shelter from the storm, a shade from the heat, for the breath of the ruthless is like a storm against a wall. The defenders are the heroes who reflect Jesus Christ*" (Isaiah 25:4, ESV).

Why God Needs Men to Defend

In the abuse recovery field, there is a great need for more Godly individuals, especially men, to take a strong vocal stance against abuse. God created the fullest set of the traits of His loving character to be exhibited through both men and women together. However, though men and women are equal in dignity and value, there is no avoiding the fact that men have a unique capacity to influence the picture women and children hold of God's character in a very powerful way.

When the devil works in the heart of men to perpetrate abuse, abandonment, addiction, assault, the image of God's character is warped among those who are experiencing or observing it. From that point onward, the child or adult will need additional healing in order to view God's character in a healthy way.

Because they often hold positions of spiritual, physical and emotional power, men usually have unique power to destroy women's and children's perception of God. Men also have the power to do something matchless to restore the image of God in the minds of women and children, as well as other men, who have been abused by men. Men who stand up and show the protective and love-filled character of Christ to the women, children, and other vulnerable ones around them are repairing the broken image of God in the hearts of the wounded.

"The greatest want of the world is the want of men—men who will not be bought or sold, men who in their inmost souls are true and honest, men who do not fear to call sin by its right name, men whose conscience is as true to duty as the needle to the pole, men who will stand for the right though the heavens fall."[1]

The Narcissism Spectrum

When men intentionally show the character of Christ to women, children, and other vulnerable people around them, they are participating in the repair of God's broken image in the hearts of the wounded. Ephesians 5's command for wives to submit to husbands is often twisted to represent forced submission on the part of women. Preachers tend to leave out the part that says, "Husbands, love your wives as Christ loved the church and gave Himself up for her."

How did Christ love the church?

How did He give Himself up for her?

Jesus set aside Himself, his identity, His power, His status, to serve His bride—to save, to rescue, and to defend her. That's the foundational principle that everything else hinges on in a God-honoring male/female relationship.

True leadership begins with selflessly serving others. A servant-leader sacrifices himself for the ones he leads. Godly leadership is rooted in reflecting the character of God and rejecting the aspects of power-over and self-exaltation shown by Lucifer.

The character of Christ is all-give. But the character of Lucifer is all-take. If you place Christ and Lucifer on opposite ends of a narcissistic spectrum, we all fall somewhere between extreme unselfishness and extreme selfishness. None but Christ are fully free of self-focus. But the more we let God's thoughts and feelings take over our human heart and mind, the more we become willing to let go of a narcissistic, me-first attitude.

Servant leadership doesn't always mean going last, either. Rather, it means acting for the good of those being served, as Jesus did. That means being first through the gate of danger: first to love, first to give, first to die. When Christian men show love in the ways that Christ loves His church, they become healers and defenders.

All power given by God is for the purpose of protecting others, never for the purpose of exploiting or oppressing them. Every human holds greater power in relative proportion to someone else in our lives. If you are an adult, you have greater power than children. If you're 16, you have greater power than a six-year-old. The problem is not the existence of a differential of power. The problem arises when power is used to exploit instead of to protect.

"He humbled himself and became obedient to the point of death, even the death of the cross. Therefore, God also has highly exalted Him and given Him the name which is above every name" (Philippians 2:8-9).

True servant leadership recognizes that all honor or authority comes from sacrifice. Faith communities typically have this upside-down. Strong religious leadership often looks like dictatorship, which is exactly the opposite of servant-heartedness. Dictatorship employs tactics such as coercion, threats, intimidation, emotional abuse, isolating, minimizing, denying, or blaming. These elements can be present in a home, a workplace, a community, or even a church.

In contrast, servant leadership looks like negotiation and fairness, non-threatening freewill choice, mutual respect, trust and support, honesty and accountability, responsible parenting, and shared responsibility.

Understanding the 13 Patterns of Abuse

Next, let's look at how the patterns of abuse play out in real life. Though this book has an emphasis on sexual abuse, Sarah McDugal has documented 12 fundamental patterns of abuse, which all revolve around a thirteenth pattern: the core attitude of entitlement and the right to take power over another person.

Before we delve deeper, it is important to acknowledge that every human alive has the capacity to be abusive, given the right circumstances. If we define abuse purely as a single action or one discrete occurrence of a behavior, then every time you behave badly, you could be labeled an abuser. That isn't how abuse is defined. People don't automatically become abusers every time they feel self-centered or act impatient.

Rather, as we discuss later in this chapter, abuse is defined as a system or pattern of behaviors in which someone with greater power uses their advantage to exploit or cause harm to someone with lesser power. When a system of persistent power exploitation exists, now you are dealing with an abuser.

If the following 13 categories of exploitation are recurring and persistent, it is safe to conclude that you are dealing with some level of an abusive system, regardless of whether it exists in a home, a church, or even the workplace.

As an advocate, a defender, or a healer, you may encounter individuals who are suffering but cannot clearly articulate what is happening and how. They may say something like, "You know, it's just really difficult. I'm not sure I'm in an abusive relationship, but things just aren't okay."

You can respond: "Look at this list of Abuse Patterns, watch a video explaining it[2], and tally each of the things that apply to you or that make you think of something similar that you've experienced."

Then you can go on to explain, "If you're in the middle of trauma fog, it can be very hard to make a complete list of all the things that you've been through and that have been used against you because this has become your 'normal.' But look through this list. If you see aspects of your own experience here, you may be in an abusive relationship."

Let's go through these one by one. Most are written with

the perspective that the victim is the spouse of the abuser but can be adjusted as necessary.

Child Abuse

- Threatens to harm children
- Doesn't pay child support
- Belittles you in front of kids
- Leverages kids to keep you silent
- Abuses other people's children
- Scares or hurts you in front of kids

Harming a child's mother is an often-overlooked aspect of child abuse, which causes trauma to the child. Lundy Bancroft explains, "The abusive man is focused on power and control, and may ignore the harm he causes the children in his desperate race to settle old scores...out of a lack of respect for the mother's humanity."

Cultural Abuse

- Mistreats you and blames it on culture
- Demeans your heritage
- Forces you to embrace their culture
- Isolates you from mainstream culture
- Uses expectations or shame to keep you silent
- Isolates you through language barriers
- Insults your family culture as inferior to theirs

Cultural abuse is especially likely in cross-cultural marriages or among those living outside of their culture of origin, where it is easier to intentionally cause isolation and limitation. An example of cultural abuse might be when everyone in the abuser's family can speak the victim's language, but deliberately speaks another language every time they get together, leaving the victim sitting alone.

Emotional Abuse

- Invalidates your perception of reality
- Insults you then says, "I'm joking!"
- Denies affection, goes silent
- Manipulates with false guilt
- Flips arguments back on you
- Acts possessive (calls it protective)
- Vacillates - creates relationship rollercoaster
- Blames you for things that aren't your fault
- Refuses to take responsibility for what they did
- Says "sorry" and promises to change, but doesn't
- Withholds nonsexual affection

Often in abuse situations, the victim has a far more tender conscience than the abuser. Victims may be conditioned (by culture, family of origin, or their abusers) to feel intense guilt, whether or not something was actually their responsibility. False guilt can be masterfully weaponized by a manipulative person.

. . .

Financial Abuse

- Limits your money
- Refuses to share accounts
- Tracks every penny you spend
- Avoids child support payments
- Spends impulsively, incurs debts
- Interferes with welfare or state aid
- Makes all financial decisions
- Lies about money, time, activities

Many abuse victims do not realize that controlling money, restricting access to the family budget, or incurring secret debt is a form of abuse. If victims are too broke to leave, then of course, they are less likely to find freedom.

Intellectual Abuse

- Demands perfection
- Insists on proof of your right to opinions
- Insults your intellect or education
- Dumbs you down
- Intimidated by your mind
- Attacks your ideas, devalues your convictions
- Refuses to allow you to disagree
- Manipulates information flow
- Invalidates others if they point out abusive behaviors
- Judges *others* for small mistakes but gives *self* grace for moral failures or rule-breaking

Double standards are common—abusers tend to be quick to judge others for small mistakes, but give themselves grace for things that are actually moral failures. For example, the abuser might lie to a police officer when he gets pulled over for speeding, but berate the victim because she didn't load the dishwasher "correctly." The minor issue is treated as a huge problem, while law-breaking is no big deal.

Pets and Property Abuse

- Confiscates your keys/ID/Driver's License
- Damages your car, refuses to keep it maintained
- Trashes your favorite things, says it was accidental
- Harms your pets, gives them away
- Punches walls, slams doors
- Controls your access to electronics
- Threatens to do any of the above

One military family was posted overseas and the wife couldn't speak or read the local language, leaving her dependent on GPS to run errands and buy groceries. Her husband blamed her if she didn't have fresh produce, but the GPS kept vanishing. One morning she overheard her daughter ask daddy why he was taking the GPS. "I'm teaching Mommy a lesson," he replied.

Physical Abuse

- Drives recklessly, road rage
- Disturbs your sleep
- Chokes, restrains, controls breath
- Blocks exits, won't let you leave
- Prevents you from getting medical care
- Throws things, uses items other than hands to cause pain or fear
- Slap/hit/kick/punch/bite/pinch/spit
- Locks you out of the house, makes you sleep outside
- Doesn't control own strength when being playful, is indifferent to pain caused
- Postures aggressively to intimidate you

"A study of 300 "choking" cases by the Family Justice Center Alliance in San Diego and Institute on Strangulation Prevention showed that a woman who is strangled even once is 750 percent more likely to be strangled again and 800 percent more likely to be killed later," writes Brian Bennett, instructor at the South Carolina Criminal Justice Academy.

Psychological Abuse

- Gaslights you — says or does things, denies it later
- Terrorizes you — then acts like it never happened
- Controls minute aspects of your life — food, fun, friends, etc
- Projects responsibility for addictions onto you or others

- Claims you misunderstood when you quote back their threats
- Displaying weapons as a way to keep you afraid
- Convinces you they know better than you do
- Controls your access to food, freedom to eat
- Tells bold *or* white lies
- Reverses questions to make you feel paranoid
- Demonstrates lack of empathy
- Can't discern your emotions accurately
- Threatens to hurt or kill themselves or others

Spiritual leaders often ask about physical abuse but aren't trained to ask other questions as well. The wife may answer, "He hasn't hit me since I was pregnant with our first child." The pastor thinks, "Great, that's not so bad!" But in reality, the abuser established his capability for violence early on. Since then, he has never needed to hit her. All he has to do is lift his shoulder in that threatening way—and she acquiesces in fear.

Psychological abusers possess a shocking willingness to commit to a lie in the face of known evidence. Against all evidence, they will still say, "That's false." If the victim has a recording of the abuser saying something, the abuser will accuse the victim of faking it. Even if there's a letter written in the abuser's own handwriting, they will insist somebody must have forged it. The more pathological an abuser's narcissism has become, the more he will commit to a big, bold lie with such passion that victims and defenders even begin to doubt their own sanity. Why? Because abusers are generally far more committed to their lie than others are to the truth.

. . .

Sexual Abuse

- Forces or withholds sex
- Criticizes your body or sexuality
- Demands sex as payment
- Uses pornography or makes you use porn
- Has affairs or threatens to cheat
- Pays for sexual services from others
- Shares sexual fantasies about others/your friends
- Lacks intimacy and connection
- Sexually abuses or molests others

Pornography is not only fornication or adultery with the person on the screen, but the porn industry is inextricably tied to sex trafficking and exploitation. In addition, porn use contributes directly to disengagement and lack of intimacy in real-life relationships.

Social Abuse

- Monitors your communication (phone, email, text)
- Tracks your social media
- Monitors your mileage
- Discourages friendships
- Dictates freedom for education/employment
- Obsesses on body image and appearance
- Limits equal social access
- Expects others to keep secrets, maintains glossy public image regardless of reality
- Keeps you at home

Many women say they had to beg for permission to go back to school or to get a job. Often, however, social abuse is more covert and insidious, and may dovetail with spiritual abuse by using Scripture to justify keeping the victim at home or avoiding friends because the abuser does not approve of their influence.

Spiritual Abuse

- Twists Scripture to avoid accountability
- Uses beliefs to gain advantage
- Leverages spiritual leaders against you
- Silences you with Bible verses
- Puts down your convictions or beliefs
- Isolates you from faith community
- Dictates your access to counseling/mentorship
- Believes you need them to teach you about God
- Soul-destroying behaviors

Refusing to discuss marital challenges with wise mentors or to get counseling from qualified professionals is a common form of spiritual abuse. Also, scriptural passages may be used to justify power over others rather than focusing on servant leadership.

Verbal Abuse

- Tells you how to do everything

- Cuts you off in conversation
- Puts you down
- Forbids you from talking to others about issues
- Monitors your conversations with others
- Shames, silences, or insults you
- Ridicules your appearance, abilities, etc
- Jokes condescendingly toward others
- Intimidates you with words and tone
- Yells/screams/swears/calls you names
- Demands that you keep secrets

One abusive pastor held small-group Bible studies in his home. He listened engagingly to guests but if his wife dared to join the conversation, he would motion for her to wrap it up in front of everyone, or verbally silence her.

(For shareable infographics on patterns of abuse, see http://sarahmcdugal.com/resources/. To compare patterns of abuse with healthy patterns of love, see the Love and Honor Wheel in Additional Resources.)

Core Mindset of Power Abuse and Entitlement

- Creates chaos — gains control by turning people against each other
- Credit hog — takes other's ideas, doesn't share glory
- Delusions of grandeur — believes they're smarter/wiser/stronger/more powerful than reality

- Dictates belief system for everyone in the household
- Entitled — acts as if others should give way to their preferences, or take care of their needs
- Supremacist — looks down on culture, color, gender, age, status, thinks own identity is superior
- Obsessed with "respect" — may get aggressive to peers/children/elderly who act with perceived disrespect
- Fixated on appearances — expects others to keep secrets, maintain glossy public image regardless of reality

Attitude of Entitlement

All forms of abuse flow from a core sense of entitlement to power and control. Those who believe that their identity (whether race, gender, culture, belief system) is superior to others are likely to develop a mindset that they have the right to dominate those beneath them. Those obsessed with power over others may take personal offense when peers, children, or even the elderly don't show them "appropriate respect." Seeking to establish control over others is not only contrary to the servant-heartedness Christ illustrates in the Gospel, but results in abusive behaviors.

Behavior Modification Does Not Fix the Problem

It is easy to hope that an abusive situation will be defused through counseling with a spiritual advisor, attending anger management, or setting up peer accountability. However, this mistaken assumption is based on a flawed understanding of what causes abuse. Contrary to popular thought, abusers do not suffer from anger management issues. They can control their anger perfectly well whenever someone important is watching. In fact, studies show that when abusers are sent to anger management classes, "wife abuse is not necessarily anger-driven, but more the consequence of a socially imposed "need" to control women," and "batterers readily reduce anger control to a set of gimmicks that enables them to get their way less violently while continuing their abuse."[3]

The perpetrator is usually more popular and powerful, especially in comparison with the victim. All the perpetrator asks is for onlookers to look away, maintain the status quo, and do nothing. This is far easier for the typical bystander than wading into the victim's mess to sort fact from fiction.

As a defender of the vulnerable, you may be accused of gossiping, but character referencing is not gossip. Even the Apostle Paul spoke clearly to protect others when he said, "Alexander the coppersmith did me much harm. May the Lord repay him according to his works" (1 Timothy 4:14,15). Speaking openly about abuse, transparently handling situations, and giving honest reports on those situations is not gossip, backbiting, or slander. It's responsible, mature behavior. Nor is speaking up "airing the dirty laundry of the church." Responsible handling of intra-church problems will not destroy the organization. It will give evidence of its well-governed, transparent manner of operation.

Consider this: What gives a better witness to people outside the faith community? To realize that sinful people did sinful things in a church filled with humans—and the church addressed it? Or to discover that sinful humans did sinful acts in a church, and then all those humans picked up the rug, collectively swept the evidence underneath, and then waited, hoping no journalist would find out?

Knowing that the church stands against abuse and takes public action against it reassures the secular world that those who claim to follow Christ are not frauds. It sends the message that believers are trustworthy and truly care about the vulnerable.

The Halo Effect

When someone has an outstanding public reputation, people tend to think they must be all good, because the public part is excellent. That's called the *halo effect*. It leads people to assume the pervasive goodness of a person on the basis of one good part. When we apply the halo effect to spiritual leaders accused of abuse, we do the entire body of Christ a huge disservice. We also deny the Bible, for it says, "The heart is deceitful above all things and desperately wicked, who can know it?" (Jeremiah 17:9). If we dismiss abuse allegations simply because someone is a fantastic preacher or a terrific evangelist or a gifted musician, we draw back in cowardice from knowing the truth. A person may have wonderful public gifts and a winning demeanor, and even do great acts of kindness, and still be capable of great evil.

As defenders enter into the work of defending the vulnerable, they will face opposition. Even strong heroes need protection. Well, you have it. We pray unceasingly for those defenders who are standing in the gap. "No weapon that is fashioned against you shall succeed, and you shall confute every tongue that rises against you in judgment" (Isaiah 54:17, ESV). "He reached down from heaven and rescued me. He drew me out of the deep waters. He rescued me from my powerful enemies, from those who hated me and were too strong for me... He led me to a place of safety" (Psalm 18:16-19, NLT). God is by your side, defenders. Go forth boldly in love.

DISCUSSION QUESTIONS

1. Think of a time when a godly man's actions helped to heal your fractured picture of God. How did it make you feel?

2. If you honestly assess yourself, where do you think you might fall on the narcissism spectrum?

3. In what ways does a biblical approach to narcissism (calling it *advanced sin*, rather than a disease) change your perception of narcissists?

4. How would you help someone who is in a difficult marriage figure out whether it's simply challenging or legitimately abusive?

5. Which of the 13 patterns of abuse was most familiar to you? Which was the least? Why?

6. Which form of abuse stood out to you as the most disturbing, and why?

7. In what ways does the concept that "all abuse comes from misplaced entitlement to power" affect your understanding of the more obvious forms of abuse?

8. Describe in your own words how identifying sin and referencing character is different from sinful gossip.

9. Why does the world outside the faith community need to see and hear the church taking action on abuse?

10. Have you ever seen the Halo Effect in action? How did the situation turn out?

7

WHEN ABUSE COMES TO CHURCH

Jesus spoke very strongly about the abuse of vulnerable people. He said, "Whoever causes one of these little ones who believe in Me to stumble, it would be better for him if a millstone were hung around his neck, and he were thrown into the sea" (Mark 9:42). "Little ones" is from the Greek word *micros* and can mean anyone who is weaker—physically, socially, financially, psychologically, experientially, or intellectually—and especially refers to those new to the faith. Jesus said that people who abuse vulnerable ones deserve capital punishment by drowning.

The "little ones" who experience abuse may have several characteristics:

- A history of being abused
- Lack of social support
- Low self-worth
- Home life trouble
- Unsatisfied longings for love
- Unhealthy fear of authority

MCDUGAL, SCHWIRZER, PARKER

Abuse perpetrators have "antennae" for weaknesses, and they often target apparently vulnerable individuals. In addition to such individuals being more likely to comply with abuse, they have less social capital in the church. Sometimes they're new to the church; sometimes they're marginalized because of their weaknesses or socioeconomic disadvantages (such as race, weight, or gender); sometimes they're unpopular. If such disadvantaged people complain about being abused by a leader, they're less likely to be believed.

Why Little Ones Don't Speak Up

Typically, victims of abuse don't speak up because they see the cost as too high. Consider these facts: The FBI estimates false reports of rape between 2 and 10 percent.[1] The Bureau of Justice estimates that only 35 percent of sexual assaults are reported to the police. (To help a person report a rape, see "H.E.L.P. for Sexual Assault Victims" in Additional Resources.) Only 14% of those reports lead to arrest.[2] That would be only 5% of the total rapes. Only 1.8% of reports result in conviction—or 0.63 percent of the total. Only 1.5 percent of reported rapes result in incarceration—only 0.53 percent of the total number of rapes. In other words, only about *one out of every two hundred rapists* ends up in jail.

The matter of whether to believe abuse allegations or not is nuanced. The odds are strongly in favor of reporters telling the truth. Only rare individuals and situations produce lies. Mental illness will sometimes lead to either imagining or lying about abuse (although abusers often target the mentally ill because they are less likely to be believed). Or a person may be bitter against someone and want to harm them through a false accusation. However, the high odds that the reporter is telling the truth should never be presented as sufficient proof of abuse. Decisions must be made according to evidence, not odds.

We must identify false allegations as what they really are—another form of abuse, what we might call "reputational" abuse. We must treat respondents (those accused of abusing) as innocent until proven guilty. If we overcompensate for perpetrator bias with a victim bias, we may commit the same error on the other extreme. Lives have been ruined through false accusations.

We may empathize and believe a reporter on their witness alone, but we also need to do a thorough investigation in every situation. In many cases it will be appropriate to take precautionary action, such as a leader stepping down during the investigation. We need to make a thorough investigation before coming to any firm conclusions. We should bear in mind that 'witnesses' can be physical evidences such as evidence of assault, or written evidence such as texts and emails, or recorded evidence such as a recorded conversations or confiscated electronics. Because rape almost never occurs in public, we can't expect "witnesses" to be actual people who saw it happen. This is partly why we strongly urge rape victims to receive a medical exam (See page 155).

Witnesses don't have to be other victims or people who saw the assault happen. A witness could be:

- A document that proves the abuse
- A recording or video
- Other physical proof that the abuse occurred
- Anyone who saw or heard the abuse

- A pattern of similar behaviors from other situations

Why Women (and Others) Sometimes Don't Fight Back

Many victims don't fight back during a sexual assault. Some think this proves they "wanted it." But careful consideration reveals a different story. Many victims experience a freeze response to assault—a sort of nervous system shutdown where they are emotionally paralyzed and unable to fight. A study from Sweden showed that two-thirds of women experience a type of paralysis known as "tonic immobility" while being assaulted. Women with trauma histories were more likely to suffer from this immobility, and those who responded by freezing were also more likely to suffer subsequent PTSD and depression.[3]

Because women tend to be smaller and physically weaker, and because of social conditioning, often they must be taught to be assertive. The Hebrew parents very likely trained their daughters to fight abuse with all their might. The law of Moses stated that if a married or betrothed woman in a populated area didn't cry out when being sexually assaulted, the elders would judge her guilty of adultery (assuming it was a secret tryst with a boyfriend), and she would be stoned (Deuteronomy 22:23-24). But if she claimed to have been assaulted in the countryside, where no one could have heard her cry, she would be considered innocent (Deuteronomy 22:25-27). Apparently Hebrew men were trained to defend a woman in trouble. This makes sense, given that Jews valued women for many reasons (such as their ability to bear children to a growing nation). Every seven years, the elders read the law of Moses in its entirety to all of Israel. This was to train every man, woman, and child regarding how to respond to assault. Women in Israel knew that if they cried out, every man within earshot knew they were to be rescued. God designed that the parents and guardians of young women would empower them to protest abuse. He also wanted men to be taught to protect young women.

Reading through the lens of some warped interpretations of the Bible might seem to indicate that blaming victims was acceptable. But we must consider the fact that the culture, environment, and training of women is different now. (Tamar, for example, said that Amnon's decision not to marry her was worse than his decision to rape her, a fact that would baffle most rape victims in our culture.) We must never blame victims for not fighting or not being assertive enough.

Some studies show that "If women fight back, their odds of being raped are cut in half, but their odds of being injured are raised by 10 percent."[4] Women faced with violent sexual assault must choose between being raped or being injured and possibly also raped. No one should fault them for either choice in this "pick your poison" dilemma.

At the same time, we must help potential victims learn new skills. There's a difference between victim-blaming and potential-victim training. Potential-victim training and a culture of support can help to prevent abuse. The church should be this type of culture.

It should be noted that male victims also often do not fight back. A number of factors feed into this, including the fact that males often experience physical stimulation that they may interpret to mean that they were complicit or enjoyed the abuse. Males also may experience even more shame and fear of being discovered, particularly if the abuser is also male. Abusers often count on this, and may tailor their grooming to keep male victims silent.

An Affair with the Pastor?

Often when a pastor has a sexual encounter with a congregant, the church members call it "an affair." We object to this label on the basis that the pastor or other spiritual leader has a clear power advantage over a congregant, thus placing a sexual encounter in the "power abuse" category.

We have designed the Spectrum of Abuse for the purpose of analyzing how much responsibility the victim may have. (See Additional Resources.) This tool will help us determine the level of victimization in a relationship that may include some culpability on the part of the victim. It is possible to be a victim and yet bear some responsibility. For instance, if a congregant is an adult who willingly engages in sex with a pastor, the pastor has clearly taken advantage of his office and of the congregant—but the congregant bears some responsibility as well.

The story of Mary Magdalene gives us one of the best illustrations of this principle. Jesus made it clear in a parable that Simon the Pharisee bore ten times as much guilt as she did. Yet her sins were "many" (Luke 7:47). Not all victims can be assumed to be 100 percent innocent. Assuming so will only hurt our cause in the end. Victims themselves may be less likely to testify if they think they'll be shirking responsibility for their part.

Sexual intimacy with a congregant is always an abuse of the office of a spiritual leader, and often abuse of the individual, too. It is most certainly taking advantage of the congregant, because the clergy person possesses a power advantage. We must also factor in the reality that women (especially those who feel powerless) are sometimes attracted to men in authority. An abusive pastor may exploit this natural sinful tendency.

These principles apply in ministries led by a spiritual leader who may not be an ordained clergyman. They apply to elders, teachers, coaches, chaplains, canvassing team leaders, and those in other leadership positions. When there is a power advantage used in a harmful way, there is power abuse. For women and children, an authority figure can be very difficult to resist.

The Appropriate Church Response

While any child abuse must be reported to the state, and while abuse between adults may also become a legal matter, God calls the church to exercise judgment on cases of abuse, too. Paul said, "Do you not know that the saints will judge the world? And if the world will be judged by you, are you unworthy to judge the smallest matters? Do you not know that we shall judge angels? How much more, things that pertain to this life?" (1 Corinthians 6:2-3). God calls the church to exercise judgment in matters of injustice within our church family.

In one case involving a church member's immoral relationship with his mother-in-law, Paul said, "Deliver such a one to Satan for the destruction of the flesh, that his spirit may be saved in the day of the Lord Jesus . . . A little leaven leavens the whole lump . . . therefore, purge out the old leaven" (1

Corinthians 5:5-7). Notice that the discipline of this man was so that he might be "saved." For the sake of the perpetrator, the victim(s), and all others, the church is called to discipline the perpetrator.

The church must certainly comply with the laws of the land that pertain to abuse. But some cases of abuse, such as a "consenting" relationship between a pastor and a non-minor congregant, are not criminally prosecutable. Still, the church has a higher standard than the world. The world addresses legal matters; the church must address moral matters, for the sake of the salvation for all concerned.

Sexual abusers in spiritual leadership should be disciplined through an evidence-based process, a process that should, in most cases, not be handled in secrecy. Consider Paul's counsel to Timothy: "Do not receive an accusation against an elder except from two or three witnesses. Those who are sinning, rebuke in the presence of all, that the rest also may fear" (1 Timothy 5:19-20). The original word for "rebuke" can mean a formal process of discipline. Often the wounds of victims of abuse will only heal if the community acknowledges the abuser's sin.

Some complain that this would be unkind to the guilty leader. We must remember that godly love looks and acts differently in different situations. Love isn't always "nice," as the world defines nice. We're told: "On some have compassion, making a distinction; but others save with fear, pulling them out of the fire, hating even the garment defiled by the flesh" (Jude 1:22-23). Isaiah said, "Your kindness to the wicked does not make them do good. Although others do right, the wicked keep doing wrong and take no notice of the Lord's majesty" (Isaiah 26:10, NLT). Unrepentant sin requires consequences because sinners become numb to God's power and authority.

Paul wrote to the Ephesians, "Let there be no sexual immorality or impurity among you. Such sins have no place among God's people. Obscene stories, foolish talk, and coarse jokes—these are not for you. No immoral person will inherit the Kingdom of Christ and of God. Don't be fooled by those who try to excuse these sins, for the anger of God will fall on all who disobey him" (Ephesians 5:3-6, NLT). We should never excuse immorality or others' excusing of it. Unaddressed sexual sin will keep the perpetrator out of heaven, and it is cruel to overlook it.

The matter of whether or not a spiritual leader should be removed from office involves much prayer and weighing of variables. If a pastor or other spiritual leader sexually abuses, however, immediate firing will give a clear message to those who might need one, and will help deter other potential perpetrators. In the case of King David, God left him on the throne in spite of his power abuse of Bathsheba and murder of her husband. Yet as king of Israel, which was a theocracy, David answered to no higher authority than God Himself. No such monopoly on power exists today. Pastors and other church leaders answer to the governing body.

David repented deeply of his sin and made no attempt to cover it up. In fact, he said, "When I kept silent, my bones grew old through my groaning all the day long" (Psalm 32:3). After the prophet Nathan confronted David, the king humbled his heart and sought the Lord, who gave him deep repentance. Then he gave evidence of that repentance over and over again before all of Israel: "Thus in a sacred song to be sung in the public assemblies of his people... which would preserve to the latest generation the knowledge of his fall, the king of Israel recounted his sin, his repentance, and his hope of pardon through the mercy of God. Instead of endeavoring to conceal his guilt, he desired that others might be instructed by the sad history of his fall."[5]

Reconciliation

Should we encourage reconciliation between repentant perpetrators and victims? Reconciliation between the abuser and the victim should not be suggested, encouraged, or recommended without qualified professional intervention, and consistent, strong evidence of attitude and behavior change. Even then, the choice belongs to the victim. When a person's will has been violated by abuse, pressuring them into reconciliation will often re-traumatize. Reconciliation implies trust, and when people have proven themselves untrustworthy to such a profound extent, offering them trust again may also only tempt abusers to return to sin.

Psalm 82 Initiative, an advocacy training organization, says, "Pastors: when a victim is pessimistic and slow to accept verbal indications of change, they are on the right track. Words are cheap, and a wise victim will not accept anything less than demonstrated repentance over time. When their abuser asks if it is righteous for them to get a second chance, you are being triangulated. Before mistaking the victim's hesitance as a lack of forgiveness you need to know that it is more likely that the abuser is asking for a 20,475th chance. You are the latecomer to the party, and you should proceed with great caution."[6]

We're told to "Execute judgment and righteousness, and deliver the plundered out of the hand of the oppressor. Do no wrong and do no violence to the stranger, the fatherless, or the widow, nor shed innocent blood in this place" (Jeremiah 22:3). "The Lord executes righteousness and judgment for all that are oppressed" (Psalm 103:6). Following in His footsteps, we will "speak up for those who cannot speak for themselves, for the rights of all who are destitute. Speak up and judge fairly; defend the rights of the poor and needy" (Proverbs 31:8-9, NIV).

DISCUSSION QUESTIONS

1. Describe what you think Jesus meant by "little ones."

2. What kind of emotions do you think Jesus felt when He said those who harm little ones deserve capital punishment?

3. What is the significance of the fact that Jesus' teaching on "little ones" precedes the teaching about going to a brother alone? How might a "little ones" situation differ from a "brother" situation?

4. What effect does a false testimony have within the community?

5. What often keeps a woman from fighting during a sexual assault?

6. What would you call a sexual relationship between a pastor and a congregant?

7. What does the story of Mary Magdalene teach about sinning in the context of being sinned against? Does a person have to be 100 percent innocent to have been victimized?

8. What redemptive message is God giving to a leader through rebuke?

9. What effects do the church's apathy and lack of discipline for the leader have upon the victim?

10. How did King David show accountability for his sin? What effect do you think this had?

HANDLING CRIMINAL ABUSE

No one ever wants to be forced to face a criminal abuse situation; however, in today's world, there is a high possibility that one day, you'll need to take action to protect a vulnerable person. When this happens, we don't want to be caught without appropriate policies in place that guide our process toward the twin goals of biblical redemption and legal responsibility.

However, while abuse policies are vital, policies are simply not enough to make a church safe. In this chapter, we will discuss practical strategies to back up your organization's policies.

Three Categories of Severity

When faced with an abuse situation, determine first which categories apply. There are three primary categories of abusive exploitation of others: 1) criminal, 2) civil, and 3) moral.

. . .

Criminal

When do you report to law enforcement? Civilians do not have the legal right to decide whether or not something is a credible evidence of abuse.

When a minor is involved, rape, sexual assault, sexual harassment, and any form of sexual contact are criminal and must be reported. (To help report a sexual assault, see "H.E.L.P. for Sexual Assault Victims" in Additional Resources.)

Know your state's age of consent. States vary from 16-18 years old on the legal age of consent for sexual activity. In most states in the US, people younger than 18 can marry with the consent of one or both parents. Some cultures may approve of "child bride" marriages and still be within the law in the US. If you're not sure of the laws, and you observe an older man taking advantage of a younger woman, report it regardless. If an abuser is known to be targeting a 16- or 17-year-old, they may have already preyed upon even younger victims.

Know your state's statutes of limitations. A statute of limitations is the length of time after a crime occurs that it can still be reported as a crime. Like ages of consent, these vary from state to state. Most range from 10 to 21 years for serious sex crimes. See RAINN's website for resources.

Know your state's mandatory reporting laws. If you're a pastor, a teacher, a counselor, a nurse, a doctor, or another person of recognized responsibility, you are probably a legally mandated reporter. This means you don't get to decide whether or not to report. If you have any awareness of possible abuse and you do not report, you can be held liable. In many states, *all* citizens are required to report suspicions of abuse. Church leaders are not biblically exempt from this duty. "Let everyone be subject to the governing authorities" (Romans 13: 1-5, NIV).

Know your state's criminal statutes. In all states, sexual activity with a minor is illegal. Reporting does not guarantee prosecution, however. Sometimes a district attorney will decline a case despite having evidence. Regardless, report to the authorities and put it on record. The report may corroborate other reports which lacked sufficient evidence. It may also simply go on file until another report makes criminal patterns obvious. Even if the report does not result in immediate charges, it was not a waste. At the very least, it gives the victim the message that we care.

Understand the evidentiary standards. In the USA, a criminal conviction requires evidence beyond reasonable doubt. That means there needs to be more than 85% to 90% certainty that a district attorney can convince a jury that this happened. Knowing that a jury may be ignorant of how sexual abuse or assault works, this may present a challenge.

Know when to let a victim report for themselves. If abuse is taking place with a minor, we have already discussed mandatory reporting. However, if the victim is an adult, do not take over or violate their free choice. Forcing or pressuring an adult victim to report is a form of abuse itself in that it removes the victim's sense of personal agency and dictates their course of action.

Instead, offer to accompany them to the appropriate law enforcement agency, help them get pictures of bruises, record or journal what is going on, assist in writing their statement, etc. Any chance of criminal conviction is going to require evidence beyond reasonable doubt. Document everything.

Do not rely on criminal conviction in order to take appro-

priate church action. If someone in the church commits a criminal act, it should be disciplined within the church regardless of whether a district attorney chooses to take it to trial. When someone beats up their spouse or molests a child, church policies should be followed and the guilty party should be disfellowshipped or censured, as the situation demands.

Civil

Many sexual abusers will not receive a criminal conviction, yet they may be sued for damages. This is called a civil suit. Actions that fall under civil laws must still be proven, but require a lower standard of evidence than criminal investigations, and are generally easier to pursue than criminal cases.

Rather than a burden of proof "beyond a reasonable doubt" (an 85%-90% likelihood), civil cases require an evidentiary standard of "more likely than not." Think of it as needing to prove the likelihood of abuse having happened, by 50% plus a feather.

Church leaders are not required to meet criminal evidentiary standards in order to take disciplinary action. Any case that meets civil standards of evidence should result in action by church leaders to bring appropriate consequences according to the Church Manual and the North American Division Working Policy. When there is sufficient evidence that a person has been defying the voice of the Holy Spirit, the church must take it seriously.

Loving well often means bringing discipline to inspire repentance. When a person isn't taking their sin seriously and is not showing humble, lasting signs of repentance, consequences will communicate that they need to change.

Churches say things like, "We cannot baptize or welcome a person who is smoking or drinking!" But if they sexually molest a child or assault their spouses, shouldn't the church leaders express far greater concern—as much as a camel is greater than a gnat?

Abuse is every bit as much of a church discipline issue as other lifestyle standards.

Moral

There are also forms of abuse and exploitation which do not rise to the level of civil or criminal prosecution. The standard of moral failure is not based on secular standards of law. Moral failures may not rise to the level of civil or criminal statutes for prosecution, but still transgress the benchmark of biblical integrity, covering all manner of moral variance and depravity.

Secular law will not prosecute someone for regularly watching pornography, but the church should take redemptive action. This approach to church discipline means we remove a porn-addicted person from positions of spiritual responsibility, in an effort to help them pay attention to the gravity of their addiction.

Church discipline for moral failure is a way to communicate, "We love you enough to help you recover from the grip of Satan. Your addiction is pulling you down. We are going to do everything within our power to rescue you from it, which includes removing your access to pride and power over others while you focus on healing." We enact church discipline, remove the pressure of church leadership, and commit to accountability for long enough to show that repentance and change are genuine and lasting.

Laying a Strong Foundation

Policies do not prevent abusers from abusing. But policies do provide a framework for proper response and handling when criminal abuse happens. Without policies, it is left for every leader to reinvent the wheel in every situation, and for perpetrator bias to sway the perception of those seeking to bring justice and healing.

Abuse perpetrated by a powerful person on a weaker person is not the time for a Matthew 18 conflict-resolution approach. Nor should mediators necessarily confront the abuser without important pre-work. If you sit down with the alleged perpetrator and say, "So-and-so says you touched them," you could inadvertently create an opportunity to destroy evidence or even possibly attack the victim. Jesus tells us to be "wise as serpents," not "wise as doves" (Matthew 10:16).

Jesus' prelude to His timeless counsel on reconciliation of brothers found in Matthew 18 states that anyone who harms a "little one" deserves to be drowned in the ocean. "Little one" can mean either a child or someone of lesser power. This concept of justice precedes the later passage of resolution between "brothers" who are peers or equals.

Do not warn the perpetrator. When you realize you have information that needs to be reported to state authorities, do so immediately. Do not warn anyone who might warn the perpetrator. Not even if you aren't sure they did it. Not even if it's your best friend. Not even if it's the richest or nicest or most charming person in church. Not even if the victim is so young or confused or unclear that you're not 100% sure. Make the report anyway.

Make sure the victim is safe and sheltered. For example, before you call the police to say, "I'm a teacher and my 13-year-old student reported to me today that her father has been sexually abusing her at home," make sure she is not at home where her abuser can retaliate.

Report completely. Write out all details before you call the authorities, to make sure you include everything you know. You can walk into the police station immediately and they can coach you through things they need to know, but be sure to say everything. There are limits of confidentiality, and one of them concerns child abuse. Even if the church asks you not to report something, report it anyway.

Inform your church. Once law enforcement is involved, encourage others to also report. Do not insist upon guilt or innocence of the alleged perpetrator. Depending on the nature of the case, you may need to talk with your children. Help them understand why the individual is not at church, and ask if they know anything about the person. Think back. Was your child uncomfortable around the alleged perpetrator?

Notify your conference and church administrators. Ask for help to prepare a media statement. If the case makes the news, you need to have a well-crafted statement ready in advance. Designate a media response contact and tell everyone else to forward media inquiries to them.

Follow church policies, regardless of law enforcement's decision. Even if authorities decline to prosecute (which often happens based on lack of DNA evidence, fear of trauma to the victim, or other technicalities), churches can still enact church discipline. When it is more likely than not that abuse happened, churches must take steps to protect the vulnerable. When they are fairly sure the allegations are true, they should immediately follow policies for church discipline.

Expect both victims and church to need support. Victims and witnesses will need compassion and tender care as they heal. Counseling, coaching, and other support services will be crucial to help the church process trauma. Remember, one-third of your church has experienced abuse of some kind. When they find out that someone they respected was an abuser, or a child or adult they love has been assaulted, old traumas may be resurrected. Ideally, if your region or conference will cooperate, organize an event or seminar for the entire church to heal and process with qualified therapists on hand.

The Four R's of Handling Abuse

Here are four steps every faith community should take to wisely handle abuse situations.

1. READY your church for the possibility of abuse

The first step in preparing your church to be a safe environment is to create and enforce policies. Even though policies do not always keep victims from being abused, they can serve to make your church a less enticing target for abusers. Abusers usually seek easy targets! Strong, clear policies also provide a clear framework to follow when a crisis arises, helping avoid confusion and mitigate perpetrator bias.

Policies that remain unenforced are not only useless to protect the vulnerable, but can also actually be a liability. When an abuse situation arises and those policies are not followed, the media and law enforcement will hold leaders to the policy that was on the books.

Many churches have policies they don't bother to properly implement. If a criminal predator with a record comes to church, the leaders may say, "We will have an elder meet him at the door who will stay beside him all the way through his time at church. He cannot even go to the bathroom alone. He is not allowed to sit at a potluck with young people at the table." However, if the leadership discovers a beloved member or lay leader to be a predator, they may avoid enforcing the policy because "We know he's repentant, we've known him for years, he's such a good guy," etc. Abusers count on building up trust by demonstrating good behavior, because when well-meaning people let their guard down, abusers get access to victims again. It doesn't matter how charming or influential or well-liked an abuser may be—churches *must* enforce safety policies.

When we prepare, prevent, and educate—teaching our churches that abuse happens everywhere, and can happen right under their noses—then when abuse *does* happen, there is usually substantially less trauma to victims. Victims are believed instead of silenced, and they are given support. They know when to report, and who to tell, and a process can be followed immediately. Educating adult leaders and members in a community dramatically reduces the risks of compound trauma to abuse victims. And because education *has* happened, and structures are put in place, abuse is also *less* likely to happen because predators looking for an easy target often move on to a more naïve church.

To protect children: provide books about safe and unsafe touch, preventing exposure to pornography, and how to report inappropriate situations to safe adults. Teach your church members to respect children's personal agency, even in small ways such as not forcing children to hug adults, or asking a child's permission before touching them, and never tickling or pulling kids onto laps against their will. You may be a wonderful person who would never dream of hurting a child, but when you demand for a child to give hugs, you set them up for the next guy to come along and say, "You must hug me, too." You could unwittingly groom them for someone else to exploit.

To protect adults: educate elected leaders, volunteers, and the general membership about abuse, the multiple forms of domestic violence (including those that are non-physical), and provide well-promoted options for reporting abuse. Other practical ideas include:

- Organizing trainings to help members learn how to recognize and respond to abuse.
- Discussing how to handle allegations with your leadership teams.
- Putting posters in church bathroom stalls describing aspects of abuse and how to report.
- Placing guidelines in public places that clearly state what your church does and does not allow for interacting with children.
- Preventing adults from entering the children's wing unless they are wearing a name tag showing

they are part of the children's staff and have already completed training and background checks.

Suggested template for a verified report:

Report Document

My name is (NAME), and I am (AGE) years old. I live in (PLACE) as a (OCCUPATION/etc) and I first met (PERPE-TRATOR) at (LOCATION/DATE).

This statement is my memory of the events that took place between (YEAR) and (YEAR) while I was (AGE) to (AGE).

Insert all details of the timeline/witness testimony.

End with:

I swear and affirm that this information is true and accurate to the best of my knowledge and ability.

Date/Name/Signature/Contact Details

2. RECORD the facts objectively, collecting evidence as you prepare to report

We've discussed how difficult it is to discern when a perpetrator is lying about their innocence. However, that does not mean intuition should be disregarded. Watch, listen, and inquire when you hear or see something that "seems off."

At times you may notice something inappropriate, but not inappropriate enough to take action. When that happens, continue observing more closely. If you see someone refusing to accept another person's boundaries, notice your inner alarm bells. One hug against a child's wishes doesn't mean abuse is happening. But it might be an indication of a worrisome pattern.

If you become aware of suspicious behavior:

- Speak carefully, if at all.
- Avoid anything that would warn a predator that you are watching.
- Document everything. Write down what you see and hear, and include the date, time and location— even if it is probably nothing.
- Ask questions of parents or kids or onlookers, if something seemed to be going on.

What you do not want to do is confront or alert possible criminal perpetrators. You want their first notification to be from law enforcement knocking on their door, so there is no time to destroy hard drives or wipe phones.

However, if you witness strong evidence of abuse, and a victim is under 18, do not wait to report! If you have good reason to believe something is being done to a minor, *do not investigate the situation yourself.*

Report any suspicions to CPS or law enforcement immediately, and let professionals do the investigation. State what happened. State it immediately. Write it down before you forget, before the details are hazy. Once you have reported to civil authorities, notify your church leadership that a report has been made.

Bringing an abuse situation to light in the appropriate way creates an opportunity for true healing to begin. Churches have an opportunity to restore the picture of the character of God in a powerful way to those who have been exploited.

. . .

3. REPORT the incident to civil authorities, then to church authorities

Know your local reporting requirements, and if there is any doubt, report and let the professionals investigate the details. In cases where no criminal elements are present but moral failure exists, still make a full report to church authorities immediately.

Even if you've reported to the police and they are taking a long time, or they don't seem to be doing anything—report to church leadership. If your local clergy excuses the behavior or refuses to follow policy, then report to the next highest level of denominational administration. If those leaders do not take appropriate action, report to the next higher level, and so on. If your denomination is a congregational structure, your options may be limited.

If the alleged victim has prepared a written report, it can be included, but only with their written permission.

Create an environment of safety for victims and witnesses to report. If there is one victim, there are very likely more. (Remember Salter's statistic of 50-150 victims on average before the first arrest?) Abusers exploit others because of their presupposition of entitlement to power over others, not because of dynamics with just one other person. This means that a predator often interacts with a number of targeted victims, testing them, grooming them, possibly abusing several, and they are careful to escalate with those who are most likely to stay quiet.

Over time, predators tend to become bolder. They may start abusing in front of cameras or when a parent or spouse is

MCDUGAL, SCHWIRZER, PARKER

just around the corner or even in the room, because risk increases the thrill. This boldness makes it even more terrifying for victims to report. When one finally speaks out, they may be joined by other victims, or others may say, "Finally, somebody said something. Now I don't have to talk."

As much as possible, however, when an abuse situation is uncovered or suspected, it is highly recommended that all victims be encouraged to report. In one situation, a brave young victim pressed charges, but insufficient evidence resulted in the case being dropped. In despair, the victim committed suicide. After her death, two others came forward and said, "He molested us, too." If they had come forward before, it probably would have saved the first victim's life.

Ways to create safe reporting:

- Offer an anonymous hotline number or email address
- Designate a qualified safe person at church to which those emails or calls go
- Speak openly about abuse without shaming victims

4. REFER to counseling and intervention

Refer the victim to sources of professional help and healing. (See "Counseling Resources" in Additional Resources.) The church should also offer to cover the costs of counseling for the victim, which ideally the abuser will reimburse if found guilty. It would benefit each church to have a fund allocated for counseling for anyone who is abused by a church member or affiliate. Often therapy will be covered by Medicaid or insurance, but if not, make sure the victim has access. Victims may minimize what happened to friends and observers because they are too afraid to tell parents or feel obligated to protect the abuser. But when they begin to trust a counselor, the splinter gets pulled from the wound. Now they can heal because they've told the truth. Suppression of the truth about abuse festers and causes the victim to continue cycles of depression and pain.

Regardless of whether someone is abusing children or adults, the perpetrator needs professional intervention as well. It doesn't matter if they are assaulting their spouse or sexually harassing 50-year-olds. They need to submit to batterer intervention or sexual addiction therapy in a professional and long-term context—for the abuser's sake, for the victim's sake, and to make the church a safe place. Leaving sin unaddressed allows it to grow unchecked.

The perpetrator's counselor or therapist should have access to the victim's testimony, and the perpetrator himself should be referred to a professional counselor who specializes in abuser intervention or sexual predators. Others should direct in the choice of a therapist; the therapist cannot be a friend or acquaintance, nor a lay accountability partner, of the perpetrator.

Falsehood is A Gospel Issue

Lying is a prominent theme throughout this book because lying is a critical component in all forms of abuse. Abusers lie to themselves over and over, thousands of times, to prevent being convicted by the truth of what they choose. They rationalize and ignore the voice of the Holy Spirit until they can't hear it anymore. This is why God hates a prideful heart—because pride encourages us to sin against the Holy Spirit, kicking against the pricks until we can't even feel them anymore.

Truth-telling is a central theme in the book of Revelation, too. Over and over, we are told that if we want to enter the New Jerusalem, we have to live in truth. Truth kills abuse. Truth heals victims. Truth heals perpetrators. Truth transforms. As leaders in faith communities, we are called unequivocally to uncover abuse and speak out in truth. May it never be said of us, "Where is the flock that was given to you, your beautiful sheep? What will you say when He punishes you? This is your lot. The portion of your measures from me, says the Lord, because you have forgotten me and trusted in falsehood" (Jeremiah 13:20-21, 25).

What can we do when the investigation reveals that abuse likely happened but, due to circumstances, law enforcement is unable to secure an arrest or prevent the abuser from having further access to victims? Sometimes the statute of limitations has passed, or there is not sufficient physical evidence or testimony to charge the perpetrators of the crimes alleged—or to bring them to conviction by a jury. We have already discussed how difficult it is to know when perpetrators are lying, especially when church members already have relationships with them and desperately want the allegations to turn out to be false.

However, there are times that we cannot safely "drop the subject" and resume acting as though the allegations were false. To do so will cause unspeakable harm to victims and will assist perpetrators in their efforts to silence the voice of the Holy Spirit in their consciences.

When there is more than 50% likelihood that abuse did, in fact, take place, churches are responsible to act on that information in order to protect vulnerable people and to assist abusers in the process of facing the truth. When all else fails, how should churches work to discern truth in these difficult situations? That is the topic of the next chapter.

DISCUSSION QUESTIONS

1. How familiar are you with your state's criminal statutes?
2. To whom should you report first, church or civil authorities? Why?
3. Explain your understanding of why the church should uphold discipline for moral standards, not merely criminal ones.
4. Express in your own words the difference between criminal and civil standards of evidence and how this impacts the church's handling of abuse.
5. Why should you not go directly to an accused abuser to get their side of the story?
6. How can your church or community take steps to better protect abuse victims?
7. How does Matthew 18 apply to abuse situations differently than peer conflicts?
8. Does your faith community provide counseling

funds for abuse victims? If not, how can you make this available?

9. What is your next planned education event to continue training your church leaders and members in abuse response?

10. Why is truth-telling a gospel mandate in dealing with abuse cases?

9

DISCERNING GENUINE REPENTANCE

"*For godly sorrow produces repentance leading to salvation, not to be regretted; but the sorrow of the world produces death. For observe this very thing, that you sorrowed in a godly manner: What diligence it produced in you, what clearing of yourselves, what indignation, what fear, what vehement desire, what zeal, what vindication! In all things you proved yourselves to be clear in this matter*" (2 Corinthians 7:10, 11).

Fruits We Can See

"Let's not be judgmental," the pastor cautioned. "These are only allegations of abuse, and we have to remember, we can't read his heart. The Bible says we need to hear both sides of a story before making a conclusion. In the mouth of two or three witnesses every word is to be established. He's a member of the church too, and he needs our help just as much as anybody else. And of course, Matthew 18 says we have to first talk alone with a person who is accused of something—so that means we can't ask others or take it to law enforcement yet."

MCDUGAL, SCHWIRZER, PARKER

If you are reading this book, chances are that you either already have, or are preparing to have, experience in dealing with allegations of sexual (or other) abuse or assault. After listening to the alleged victim and providing emotional and other support, you will need to assess the situation carefully. False accusations do happen, and although they are very rare (statistically only about 2-8%), we must always operate with the understanding that there is a possibility that the allegations are false, misstated, or sometimes result from a misunderstanding. Due to statutes of limitations on illegal behavior, lack of evidence, and other factors, not every allegation can be handled effectively by law enforcement. What if the alleged abuse situation happened 30 years ago, or is being reported by a third party who did not actually witness the crime but was only told of it by others? What if the person reporting changes their story the next day and denies the abuse, but there is still a significant likelihood that the abuse actually happened?

There are times that the next step after listening to allegations of abuse is to move forward with the next layer of investigation by talking with the alleged offender. (For the sake of simplicity, we will not bog readers down with the term "alleged" prefacing every mention of victims and abusers in this discussion, but keep in mind that both terms must be understood to be referring to alleged victims and alleged abusers.)

Some people firmly assert that the right thing to do is "assume the best" until we actually have solid physical proof that the abuse happened (or perhaps have multiple witnesses). But "assuming the best" is not as easy as it might sound. If the offender denies that the abuse happened, assuming the abuser is telling the truth (except in occasional cases of misunderstanding or mistaken identity) usually means assuming the victim is lying. When there is about 95% chance that the victim is telling the truth, we must be cautious about taking things at face value.

Victims are usually the ones more hesitant, quick to back down and fade away. Abusers are more likely to be confident, respected members of the community, powerful, older than victims, and often quick with a winning smile and smooth explanation. In addition, abusers are usually not easily disposable to the community (elders, pastors, teachers, etc.), and may be inclined to threaten legal action if anyone asks questions or pursues further action. In short, perpetrator bias is usually by far the easiest path for those dealing with the situation— believe the abuser unless the victim produces proof beyond reasonable doubt. After all, if the abuse can be assumed not to have happened, friendships can resume, and the community does not have to be disrupted. The potential emotional price for the victim seems small sometimes, especially in comparison to the threat of prison, public exposure, and other embarrassments to the abuser and the people and institutions related to him. These and many other factors lead investigations to usually tip toward a strong bias in favor of believing the perpetrator.

The cautions given at the beginning of this chapter are all rooted in biblical truth, and must each be taken seriously in the appropriate context. However, the Bible also says, "You will know them by their fruits" (Matthew 7:16, 17). Especially in abuse situations, these fruits may only be visible to the discerning eye. Almost all abusers do many good things. Often, the craftiest are the wolves in sheep's clothing—those intentionally pretending, rationalizing, and seeking to frost over their sins with a thick layer of apparent "righteousness." Rather than bearing actual fruits of righteousness, though, they are like gardeners anxious to make good false impressions. They earnestly work to staple pretended "fruits" on the branches of their "orchard," to convince people looking on from the outside that they are godly.

If false fruits affixed on the branches look almost exactly like genuine fruits, how can we tell the difference? We can't read hearts. It can seem discouragingly difficult to discern. Many throw their hands in the air, crying, "Only God knows. Let's just assume the best." When we respond this way, though, *we will usually be doing the wrong thing.* The actual victims of abuse will shrink away into silence, and abusers will be emboldened in their sin—perhaps forever crippled in their efforts to come to Jesus for true, soul-searching healing.

So, how can onlookers tell the difference between true and false repentance? Usually taking a closer look at the "fruits" stapled on the branches can reveal the truth. Without getting a degree in criminal law, it is still possible for the average person to develop discernment based on biblical principles. The answers often lie in taking a closer look at Scripture and applying its truths more carefully.

For the sake of instruction on the essentials of how sin and repentance work, let's go back to the inception of sin. Genesis 3 and 4 give us a skeletal outline, a bare-bones analysis of the difference between true and false repentance. While this analysis is not exhaustive, it simplifies the dramatic contrast between these two things that might sometimes appear nearly identical to a casual observer. This chart is designed to be a basic sketch of some biblical guidelines to use when evaluating the genuineness of the "fruits" of repentance, to discern true from false.

True Repentance

1. **Confess**/Apologize Completely

"If we confess our sin, He is faithful and just to forgive us our sin." 1 John 1:9

2. **Take Responsibility**

"I acknowledge my transgressions, and my sin is ever before me." Psalm 51:3

3. **Accept Consequences**/Make Restitution/Welcome Accountability

"Create in me a clean heart, O God, and renew a steadfast spirit within me." Psalm 51:11

False Repentance

1. **Hide**/Lie/Minimize

"I heard Your voice in the garden, and I was afraid because I was naked; and I hid myself." Genesis 3:10

2. **Blame**/Rationalize/Excuse

"The woman whom You gave to be with me, she gave me of the tree, and I ate." Genesis 3:12

"Am I my brother's keeper?" Genesis 4:9

3. **Play Victim**/Dodge Consequences

"My punishment is greater than I can bear!" Genesis 4:13

. . .

What do these principles look like applied in real life? Let's examine each of these categories in a bit more depth.

1. Confession vs. hiding/lying/minimizing

True offenders often flatly deny abusing. "I never would have touched her like that! I'm no pervert. People who do stuff like that should be shot." An honest person talking with the offender may find it difficult to even imagine that this person could lie so convincingly, because *they could never lie like that themselves.* This blustering approach relies on the hope that their victims lack credibility or will back down under pressure, that there are no other witnesses or further evidences, and that nothing more (such as testimonies of other victims) will come out later.

But when abusers lie outright, they risk losing all credibility. One testimony of an unseen observer or another victim, one forgotten bit of evidence, and their story is proven false. Often, a shrewder approach is to confess what they believe is already known or can be proved—plus a little more, to appear authentic (and perhaps silence their own consciences). They often do this with tears, strategically including mentions of the forgiveness of God, newfound peace, and/or remarkable transformations.

How can honesty be discerned, or even an honest confession be distinguished from one that involves hiding, minimizing, and even outright lying? Here are a few tips:

- Ask good, open-ended questions. Instead of "Did you touch her?" try "Explain what happened." Then listen closely for *any* hint of dishonesty, minimizing, or someone fishing for how much you already know.

- Be alert for vague answers and "I'm confused" questions—retorts used for the purpose of angling to find out how much is already known. Make note: You are *not* obligated to disclose what you already know about the situation. "A fool vents all his feelings, But a wise man holds them back" (Proverbs 29:11). When the alleged abuser doesn't know what you already know, they may accidentally disclose crucial information, or confirm crucial details of the reporter's story. Of course, you may want to comfort this person (who may be innocent), especially if you have a relationship with them already. But an honest person won't need to know how much you already know—they will be focused on accurately sharing what happened. Save the sympathy for later. A simple "I'm sorry this is so hard for you" is sufficient.

- After you have listened to their story, carefully bring up any discrepancies with the reporter's story. "Help me understand a little more about what happened when you walked into the living room alone with her. How far from her were you?" While there may be slight discrepancies in two people's stories even when both are telling the truth, there should be a clear agreement on basics; otherwise, someone is lying. "I was all the way on the other side of the room and never touched her" doesn't match "He was right beside me when we walked through that doorway, and then he grabbed me."

- Note dramatic descents into emotion or angry declarations of innocence. Overpowering emotion can be a way of derailing the conversation.

- Note also any attempts to manipulate that rapidly escalate into attempts to control when they are not getting what they want. A swing from friendliness when things seem to be going well to a quick "I could sue you for defamation because of that conversation!" is a sign that this person is manipulating and determined to remain in control by any means necessary. This is a clue that your questions may be getting closer to the root of the problem—or are awakening this person's fear of being found out.

- Remember, more experienced liars sometimes give excessive detail in order to make themselves sound more believable. Irrelevant details like "she was wearing a pink shirt and it had this black piece of fuzz on her lower back, so I picked it off, and maybe she misunderstood" might not be accurate.

- Document everything. You can tell the person you're taking notes because you don't trust your memory and want to make sure you have the story right (which is wise; these notes may be admissible later for testimony in court). In your notes, write down any discrepancies in the person's testimony. Come back to them later for clarity. Try to write down exactly what the person says when possible; you can underline or put exact words in quotation marks.

- If possible, have someone trustworthy present to

verify what was said (because the story may well change later, and it will be your word against theirs). Or record the conversation, if that is legal. If possible, it is better for the person not to know their testimony is being recorded, as a guilty person will often be more careful what they say, and may not slip on important details. But in some states and countries, it is illegal to record a conversation without permission from all parties involved, so check beforehand. If you have multiple witnesses, have them also document what they hear.

- Watch out for confessions that graphically admit everything except illegal activities, but vigorously deny that part of the story. These are often a ploy to maintain credibility while avoiding any serious consequences.

- In contrast, a truly repentant abuser will admit exactly what they did in its entirety, answer further questions thoroughly, and be able to explain why what they did was wrong.

2. *Taking responsibility vs. blaming, rationalizing or excusing*

Genuine repentance never excuses sin. While others involved may also bear some guilt, a truly repentant person will not look for opportunities to highlight that fact.

How can taking responsibility be distinguished from blaming and minimizing? Here are some tips:

- Recognize shrewd attempts to hold up a standard

that no one in the room has attained. "I'm not perfect" or "Of course, I'm tempted by lust sometimes" are probably attempts at minimizing.

- Don't fall for sly attempts to blame disguised as "taking responsibility." "I admit, I find some body shapes especially attractive. I take full responsibility for that, even though I guess God made me that way. So when I saw her wearing that dress..." That's *not* taking full responsibility—it's rationalization and blame.

- Watch for attempts to connect with you as a fellow sufferer, thereby minimizing the sin as merely a common temptation. "You know, sometimes I struggle with controlling my thoughts when women dress immodestly. Every normal man does, right, Pastor?" may be an attempt to water down the sin's severity, portraying it as something "everyone does." Also, watch out for coming-alongside questions that attempt to get you to side with the accused. "It was just one of those things that happen when you aren't having enough devotional time. You know how that is, right?" *Never* agree with statements like this—it helps silence the abuser's conscience and will paralyze your ability to confront later.

- Minimization will often be woven into brief, passing terminology. Pay prayerful attention to the "insignificant" statements that slip out amid the polished presentation. "In Bible times, they got married at 12" is not an explanation—it is a justification that has clearly been used to silence what is now a seared conscience. The discerning ear must recognize such statements as key clues revealing what is *actually* happening in the person's heart behind the façade. "It was just a slip" or "Perhaps I wasn't completely honest" strips away the false righteousness to reveal the naked sin still unrepented underneath. Repentant sinners don't excuse sins as "slips."

- Minimization can take the form of turning a serious fall into a "Whoops!" Sinners don't really fall into sin; we crawl into it. If a person says, "I put safeguards in place, but I guess I didn't have enough," they are making a serious sexual sin seem like a careless mistake rather than the egregious crime it is. They're not sorry yet—and likely never will be, if everyone accepts that excuse.

- As they progress up the path to healing, an abuser will demonstrate genuine repentance by showing insight into the underlying motivation from which their behavior flowed. They will also be specific in their confessions. They will do so without a shred of blaming the victim or watering down the reality with weaker words. It should sound like "I was cruel and selfish and entitled," instead of just "It was wrong of me."

3. *Accepting consequences, making restitution, and welcoming accountability vs. playing victim and dodging consequences*

Consequences are always difficult to endure, but they are the acid test of discerning genuine repentance. Consequences force a person who has recognized the harm of their sin to reevaluate whether they *really* want the painful journey of healing. Those who have heartily displayed initial signs of genuine repentance often wilt here, as the sprouts in stony ground wither because they have "no depth of earth" (Mark 4:5). Not all abusers are willing to do the hard work of repentance; many would rather lose relationships than lose power. A careful balance of encouragement and accountability is necessary to preserve the tender beginnings of genuine repentance —or reveal the lack of it. In dealing honestly with sexual abuse or assault situations, the consequences may include criminal charges. This dimension adds a heightened intensity to the temptation to lie, blame, and evade consequences. But genuine repentance will march resolutely into the storm of painful repercussions of sin, determined to become like Jesus at any cost.

How can an observer discern whether an abuser is accepting their consequences instead of playing the victim? Here are some tips:

- Ask for a handwritten confession of what the abuser did. (It can be argued later that a typed one may have been written or edited by someone else.) Does the abuser hesitate at the thought, or ask if they can talk with their lawyer first? If so, they are probably not nearly as interested in making their previous wrongs right as they are in avoiding consequences. The handwritten confession should explain what they did without leaving anything out. It should state why they did it and why it was wrong. It should include accepting responsibility, affirming that the victim did the right thing by reporting, and relinquishing of control that includes agreeing to take whatever steps are necessary to help victims heal. It should *not* include any blame, minimization, etc. If necessary, it can be used to establish their guilt later if they decide to back out of their confession. A truly repentant person will realize that taking full responsibility can reverse some of the consequences the victim is suffering. Aiding in such healing will be more important to them than dodging consequences themselves.

- Watch the initial gut reactions when you state that accountability is going to be necessary. Is the abuser cautious, wondering what will be the cost? Accountability is critical to the process of transformation. Those who have lost confidence in their own discernment and are eager to change will welcome accountability. If they are willing to do whatever it takes to purge out the former patterns, they will not make statements like, "I need help, and I'm willing to do all I can to get over this thing—but I can't put filters on my computer and phone, because those filters block all kinds of stuff I need for work/school." There are computers at the library and lots of other places. They don't need convenience and ease as much as they need rehabilitation, and accountability is a crucial step. Enough said.

- See if the abuser takes initiative to ask how to repair harms, not only to the victim but also to

others who have been indirectly hurt. Are they
offering to pay for counseling and other expenses
for their victim? Willingness to provide funds to,
as much as possible, repair the damage done is a
good sign.

- Listen for indications that the abuser is grateful for
the act of reporting, and for acknowledgements
that the victim has done the right thing by
reporting. A truly repentant abuser will be grateful
they are being given an opportunity to make things
right.

- Evaluate the abuser's approach to control. Abuse is
all about control, so the reversal of abuse
necessitates giving up control. Do they try to
control the conversation, plan out steps to take in
turning things around, or even express a desire to
take over the investigation? If so, they are not on
the path to healing yet.

- The abuser should pursue professional counseling
with individuals experienced in abuse, narcissism,
and sociopathic tendencies, and should give
evidence that they are pursuing counseling. The
abuser needs extensive help to break out of
damaging thinking patterns.

- If appropriate, inform the abuser of any criminal
investigations and of possible outcomes. While a
response of dismay is expected, again, a truly
repentant abuser will be far more interested in
doing what is right than in avoiding the just
consequences of their crimes.

- A high-profile abuser should bow out of all public

ministries or other forums likely to yield a false sense of security regarding their spiritual condition. A pastor or other spiritual leader's "drug" is the praise of the people. A person truly seeking freedom from alcohol will not visit bars; likewise, an abuser should abstain from their "narcissistic feed" for a period of time appropriate for the wrong committed. This decision should be in the hands of those seeking to hold the abuser accountable; full submission will be a sign that the abuser is truly repentant.

- A suitable accountability point-person should be found to oversee that the abuser attends counseling, provides funds for the victims' counseling, and avoids high-profile, ego-feeding appearances, and to make sure the abuser complies with other aspects of the recovery program.

Recommended Consequences for Sexual Abuse in a Church Context

Each situation is different, but as a general rule, an individual who has sexually abused in a church context should bear the following consequences:

1. Mandatory time out of the pulpit/public ministry, likely permanently, but at the very least temporarily (i.e. several years).

2. Ten or more counseling sessions by a recommended (by other people) professional counselor who understands (and if

possible, specializes in) sexual abuse psychology and abuser intervention treatment.

3. An accountability partner (recommended by other people) who oversees the abuser's compliance. This should not be a friend or someone chosen by the abuser, but someone capable of being fully objective with the offender.

4. The written testimony of the victim delineating what the abuser did should be given to both the counselor and the accountability partner. If the victim is comfortable speaking with the counselor and/or accountability partner, the offender should give written permission to both to speak freely with the victim.

5. The abuser should attend some kind of weekly accountability group. Depending upon the type and severity of the abuse, that choice can be made with the counselor.

6. Except under extraordinarily unusual circumstances, the abuser should not be allowed to contact the victim. An exception may be made for a handwritten apology that is pre-approved by the counselor.

7. Written apologies to all people harmed, as well as financial support to receive counseling and for any other damages caused by the abuser, are basic reparative measures based on the biblical principle of "restore again what he has robbed" (Ezekiel 33:15).

True or False Repentance?

The sins of Judas and Peter were similar. What followed the sin determined their very different outcomes. Judas sorrowed for the consequences of sin—the shame, the humiliation, the loss of reputation. Peter, on the other hand, tapped into a different motive. After his third denial with cursing and swearing, "The Lord turned and looked at Peter" (Luke 22:61). "In that gentle countenance he read deep pity and sorrow, but there was no anger there."[1] Peter stumbled out into the night, and finally fell on his face before God in the very garden where Jesus had sweat blood for him. It was that horrible realization of his own evil that began the process of changing Peter from a denier of Jesus to a proclaimer of Jesus. What made his repentance effective was that he looked at how his sin hurt Jesus, instead of merely dwelling upon how it hurt him.

What Does Genuine Repentance Look Like?

The most comprehensive description of true repentance is found in 2 Corinthians 7:10-11. In this passage, Paul describes the beauty of the climb toward godly sorrow for sin, contrasting it with the slide toward worldly sorrow that does nothing to bring about transformation. "For godly sorrow produces (*ergazomai*, to purposely labor or work) repentance leading to salvation, not to be regretted; but the sorrow of the world produces (*katergazomai*, to work out or effect unconsciously) death."

Notice how the development of godly sorrow into repentance is a purposeful process involving labor—in contrast to the sorrow of the world producing death, which is more of an unconscious process. This seems to indicate a certain intentionality to true repentance, versus an emotional reaction without true engagement of the will. What intentional actions does true repentance produce? Let's break down the features of repentance one at a time:

- "What diligence it produced in you" – Diligence is *speudo*, the Greek word for "speed or diligence."
- "What clearing of yourselves" – Clearing is *apologeomai,* "a speech in defense," meaning defense of the one wronged in which there was no evasion of sin or self-justification.
- "What indignation" – This is the word *aganakteó,* "indignation," referring to anger at sin, themselves, and the tempter.
- "What fear" – Here we see the word *phebomai,* "to be put to flight," to have self-distrust, and reverence.
- "What vehement desire" – This is from *epipotheó,* "longing," desire for change, for reconciliation with God, for restitution.
- "What zeal" – This is from *zeo,* "jealousy," which is anger and love combined, leading to intense purpose.
- "What vindication" – The word *ekdikeó* is used here, "avenging of wrong," or revenge for sin, restitution for wrongs done.
- Paul closes this list of descriptors with, "In all things, you proved yourselves (*sunestēsate,* 'to commend, establish, stand near, consist') to be clear (*hagios,* ("ceremonially clean, holy, sacred") in this matter.

In summary, true repentance will lead a person to an intentional, open process which includes:

- diligent, intentional avoidance of sin

- full and detailed confession of wrong
- validation of those wronged
- validation of God's laws
- anger at self, sin, and Satan
- self-distrust
- appropriate fear of God
- longing for change
- jealousy for the cause of the victim
- full financial, social, spiritual, and all forms of restitution where possible

In Conclusion

To the untrained eye, vigorous denials may be all the "evidence" required to declare accusations of sexual abuse to be false. In other situations, pretentious sobbing, apparent anguish, and declarations of new beginnings can look very similar to genuine repentance. However, genuine repentance is distinguishable by clear fruits that can and must be sought by the discerning helper. This is a critical part of gospel work, both for the sake of the victim and any other potential victims, and also for the abuser's eternal salvation. Souls hang in the balance—it is crucial that we get this right.

DISCUSSION QUESTIONS

1. The Bible presents repentance as something that bears fruits. How does carefully discerning the fruits of repentance differ from un-Christlike judgmentalism, gossip, backbiting, and criticism?

2. Why do you think God puts the responsibility for discerning the fruits of repentance upon human beings working in cooperation with His Holy Spirit, rather than just sending an angel or a sign in the heavens?

3. Of all the characteristics of true repentance, which one seems the most essential to you personally? Can you share a reason why this is so?

4. Why do you think God wants abusers to make restitution to those they've harmed?

5. As you examined the list of common evasion techniques used by unrepentant abusers, did you recognize any from experience? Please share specifics.

6. As you examined the list of ways unrepentant persons can minimize abuse, did you recognize any from experience? Please share specifics.

7. What is the purpose of refraining from telling all we know about a case to the accused, before giving them a chance to confess?

8. What are some of the ways a truly repentant person makes restitution and demonstrates that they are serious about their recovery?

9. Share a biblical example of worldly sorrow, meaning self-centered remorse for sin.

10. Share a biblical example of godly sorrow, meaning God-centered repentance for sin.

AFTERWORD

As the wise man said, "Show me a righteous ruler and I will show you a happy people. Show me a wicked ruler and I will show you a miserable people" (Proverbs 29:2, GNT). As a church family, we have the opportunity to be ruled according to God's timeless, immutable principles of righteousness, and to provide in the church the safe refuge the world so desperately needs. To that end, we dedicate this book.

ADDITIONAL RESOURCES

Abuse Response Decision Tree
Abuse Spectrum Assessment
Coaching and Courses
Counseling Resources
Support Groups
HELP for Victims of Sexual Assault
Listening Well
Other Organizations
PTSD and the ACE Test
Post-traumatic Growth Inventory
Systems of Abuse
Love & Honor Wheel
Sexual Addiction Recovery

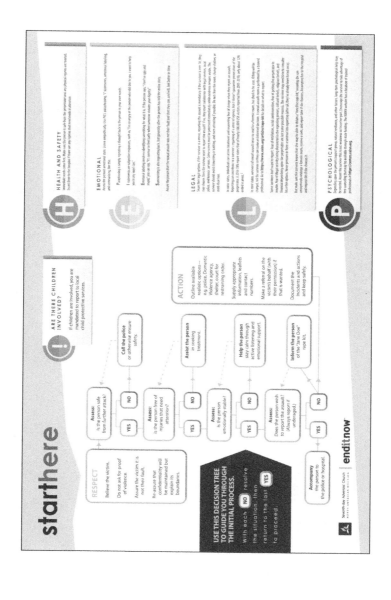

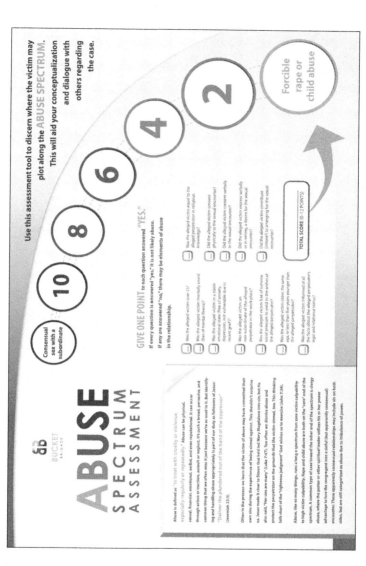

ABUSE
SPECTRUM ASSESSMENT

BUCKET BRIGADE

Use this assessment tool to discern where the victim may plot along the ABUSE SPECTRUM. This will aid your conceptualization and dialogue with others regarding the case.

Consensual sex with a subordinate → 10 → 8 → 6 → 4 → 2 → Forcible rape or child abuse

Abuse is defined as "to treat with cruelty or violence, especially regularly or repeatedly." Abuse can be physical, sexual, financial, emotional, verbal, and even reputational. It can occur through action or inaction, assault or neglect. It's such a broad, pervasive, and common thing that we often miss it just because we're so used to it. But identifying and handling abuse appropriately is part of our duty as followers of Jesus: "Deliver the plundered out of the hand of the oppressor" (Jeremiah 22:3).

Often in the process we learn that the victim of abuse may have committed their own sins during the experience of being sinned against. This shouldn't surprise us. Jesus made it clear to Simon that he'd led Mary Magdalene into sin, but He also said, "Her sins are many" (Luke 7:47). Too often we dismiss abuse and protect the perpetrator on the grounds that the victim sinned, too. This thinking falls short of the "righteous judgment" God wishes us to exercise (John 7:24).

Abuse, like so many things, runs a long a spectrum from zero victim culpability to high victim culpability. Rape and child abuse are both on the "zero" end of the spectrum. A common type of case toward the other end of the spectrum is clergy abuse, where the pastor or other spiritual leader utilizes his or her power advantage to lure the congregant into a sinful (but apparently consensual) encounter. These apparently consensual relationships may include sin on both sides, but are still categorized as abuse due to imbalance of power.

GIVE ONE POINT to each question answered "YES."

If every question is answered "yes," it is not likely abuse.

If any are answered "no," there may be elements of abuse in the relationship.

☐ Was the alleged victim over 25?

☐ Was the alleged victim mentally sound (free of mental illness)?

☐ Was the alleged victim in a stable emotional state (free of anxiety, depression, not vulnerable due to recent grief)?

☐ Was the alleged victim an non-subordinate of the alleged perpetrator in the work place?

☐ Was the alleged victim free of extreme social pressure to yield to the wishes of the alleged perpetrator?

☐ Was the alleged victim older, the same age, or less than five years younger than the alleged perpetrator?

☐ Was the alleged victim informed of all the facts about the alleged perpetrator's legal and relational status?

☐ Was the alleged victim equal to the alleged perpetrator in religious knowledge?

☐ Did the alleged victim consent physically to the sexual encounter?

☐ Did the alleged victim consent verbally to the sexual encounter?

☐ Did the alleged victim express verbally or in writing, a desire for the sexual encounter?

☐ Did the alleged victim contribute (initiate?) to arranging for the sexual encounter?

TOTAL SCORE (0-12 POINTS)

145

COACHING AND COURSES

WILD Coaching Services

Private individual sessions and group study sessions bring you encouragement and accountability as you journey toward clarity, wellness, and wholeness. Learn how to let go of false guilt, set healthy boundaries, recognize abusive patterns clearly, and step out of the trauma fog. www.wildernesstowild.com

WILD Online Courses

Affordable online courses guide your journey from victim to warrior, as you heal from abuse. Courses include topics related to abuse from spouses, parents, workplace, faith community, post-trauma wellness, managing anxiety, overcoming toxic shame, and much more. www.wildernesstowild.com

COUNSELING RESOURCES

1. Abide Counseling Network offers biblical mental health counseling and coaching via telephone and internet. Project Safe Church is a partnership between Abide Counseling and the Lake Union of Seventh-day Adventists. To find a counselor, go to abidecounseling.com and fill out the intake form. Abide also has free telephone support groups and other resources.

2. A directory of Seventh-day Adventist counselors can be found at the NAD Family Life website. Go to nadfamily.org and click on "Resources," then "Directory of Counselors."

3. The American Association of Christian Counselors has a directory at connect.aacc.net.

4. New Life Live Christian Radio has a database of counselors at newlife.com/counselors.

SUPPORT GROUPS

1. Abide Counseling Network has free telephone support groups. Details are on the web page at abidecounseling.com. Abide also has low-fee groups for abuse recovery, depression, and anxiety. Fill out the contact form and we'll give you current information.

2. Celebrate Recovery is a "Christ-centered, 12-step recovery program for anyone struggling with hurt, pain or addiction of any kind. Celebrate Recovery is a safe place to find community and freedom from the issues that are controlling our life." To find a group near you, go to celebraterecovery.com/crgroups.

3. The Seventh-day Adventist Church has a recovery group network at adventistrecoveryglobal.org.

4. There are more than 30 types of 12-step groups. These groups utilize biblical principles of recovery but aren't openly Christian. A list of the kinds of groups can be found at en.wikipedia.org/wiki/List_of_twelve-step_groups.

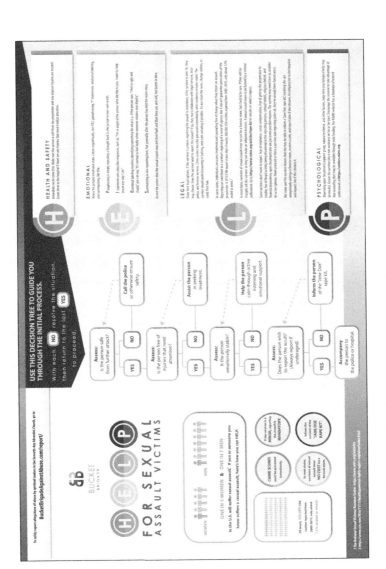

LISTENING WELL

Empathy, with its sense of connectedness and shared experience, forms a solid basis for good communication. This exercise will help us learn the skills of developing effective, empathic bonds with one another.

Remember the formula: **E**mpathy = **A**sk and **R**eflect.

Two essential components to empathic listening are **asking** questions and **reflecting** what we hear.

Asking Questions

The purpose of asking questions is to draw out the thoughts, feelings, and opinions of the other. Try to use what, where, when and how questions, as "why?" can often sound accusatory. Make sure the questions aren't veiled accusations, as in, "What made you go into that room alone with him?" Probe in more non-judgmental ways, such as, "What feelings and motivations were you experiencing at the time you entered that room?"

Reflecting

Likewise, the purpose of reflection is to draw the person out. The point of reflecting is not to agree or disagree with the person but to understand them. Simply put in your own words what you heard them say, asking them to confirm or correct. Again, the point is to understand. You're not going for the objective truth, but their subjective truth.

Reflecting can fall into three basic categories:

Mirroring is simply repeating back the last few words a person said.

Speaker: "I just can't stand it anymore!"

Listener: "You can't stand it."

Paraphrasing is putting a small amount of information into your own words.

Speaker: "I just can't stand it anymore!"

Listener: "You feel as if the whole situation with your uncle has become unbearable?"

Summarizing is digesting a larger amount of information and reviewing it with the person.

Speaker: (Tells the whole story about her uncle.) "I just can't stand it anymore!"

Listener: "So, let me make sure I have this right. When your uncle kept trying to find time alone with you, you felt weird about it, but at the same time didn't want to accuse him. You worried that your family members would be angry at you for reacting that way and that your uncle's feelings would be hurt. Your mother told you over and over growing up that your uncle, her brother, was a great person. Plus, he's a pastor and evangelist, and if you accused him, you thought the religious community might accuse you of 'bringing down a man of God." All those motivations, and your uncle's persistence, came together at that moment he asked you to go into that room with him. Now you're struggling with self-blame for what happened and dreading telling your family, but you feel as if you're living a lie and the pressure is mounting. Do I have that right?"

This simple practice of reflection can help stay focused on the conversation, help you get quickly to the core issues, and enable a person to trust and feel comfortable with you. Make sure to use as much reflection as question-asking, or even more. One question after another can seem like an interrogation and might shut the person down.

OTHER ORGANIZATIONS

Abide Counseling Network is a network of trained male and female Seventh-day Adventist counselors and coaches who provide a variety of affordable emotional and mental health resources, including Skype or phone sessions. Abide also offers regular support and helper training events for those who wish to become better equipped to serve others.

www.abidecounseling.org

Bucket Brigade Against Abuse is a support initiative of the Seventh-day Adventist church which is dedicated to bringing education, awareness, and victim support. BB provides a confidential online reporting feature for making known cases of sexual abuse perpetrated by church leaders in Adventism, and the BB team functions in cooperation with church leaders and appropriate law enforcement to take action when needed.

www.bucketbrigadeagainstabuse.com

EndItNow is an initiative of the North American Division (NAD) to educate church leaders and to raise awareness about multiple forms of abuse. The annual EndItNow Summit is live streamed and targeted for clergy awareness of abuse issues.

http://enditnow.org

Godly Response to Abuse in a Christian Environment (GRACE) is under the leadership of former prosecutor Boz Tchividjian. Their mission is "Empowering Christian communities to recognize, prevent, and respond to abuse." They provide education, information, and support for victims.

http://netgrace.org

Project: Safe Church is an initiative to bring conferences and unions into compliance with the NAD's Sexual Ethics Policy (E-87 in the NAD Working Policy), in partnership with Abide Counseling and Bucket Brigade Against Abuse (Sarah McDugal, Jennifer Schwirzer, Dr. Alan and Nicole Parker, and Paul Coneff). PSC is a training initiative to equip church leaders, pastors, administrators, and appropriate laity on how to recognize and respond to abuse in biblically redemptive yet legally responsible ways.

www.projectsafechurch.org

Psalm 82 Initiative exists to help churches and their leaders recognize and respond to abuse in the church more effectively. Psalm 82 provides coaching, education, and support to those seeking to use their power to protect and to make churches safer for the vulnerable.

https://www.patreon.com/Psalm82

Sarah McDugal is an author, speaker, and abuse recovery coach who works exclusively with female survivors of abuse. She offers training events for churches and organizations on how to recognize and respond to abuse, as well as inspirational events focused on God's love and healing for women and teen girls. McDugal offers both group and individual online coaching, available internationally, for women recovering from abuse.

www.sarahmcdugal.com

The Hope of Survivors serves victims of clergy sexual misconduct across denominations. They provide educational materials and events, and they have a website loaded with helpful information.

www.thehopeofsurvivors.com

WILD Community provides confidential and free online support groups for women recovering from abusive marriages and/or abusive parents, online training courses for development and growth after abuse, and online group coaching for spiritual and emotional healing. WILD also provides coaching services for abuse recovery, post-trauma wellness, and entrepreneurship development.

www.wildernesstowild.com

PTSD AND THE ACE TEST

Post-Traumatic Stress Disorder (PTSD)—A psychological disorder that can develop in response to a traumatic event in which there was threatened death, serious injury, or sexual violence.

Markers of PTSD:
- Nightmares: may take the form of repetitive high-stress dreams
- Flashbacks: intrusive, compulsive memories, which may be extremely vivid
- Extreme emotional reactiveness to triggers (events, experiences, memories, objects, places, or people)
- Dissociation/depersonalization: feeling distant, losing track of time, experiencing memory voids, getting lost in thought, feeling robotic

The ACE Test

Instructions: Give yourself one point for each "yes" answer.

The more "points" you have, the higher your ACE score, and the more likely you are to be continuing to deal with post-traumatic issues.

1. Before your 18th birthday, did a parent or other adult in the household often or very often... swear at you, insult you, put you down, or humiliate you? Or act in a way that made you afraid that you might be physically hurt?

2. Before your 18th birthday, did a parent or other adult in the household often or very often...push, grab, slap, or throw something at you? Or ever hit you so hard that you had marks or were injured?

3. Before your 18th birthday, did an adult or person at least five years older than you ever... touch or fondle you or have you touch their body in a sexual way? Or attempt or actually have oral, anal, or vaginal intercourse with you?

4. Before your 18th birthday, did you often or very often feel that...no one in your family loved you or thought you were important or valued? Or your family didn't look out for each other, feel close to each other, or support each other?

5. Before your 18th birthday, did you often or very often feel that...you didn't have enough to eat, had to wear dirty clothes, and had no one to protect you? Or your parents were too drunk or high to take care of you or take you to the doctor if you needed it?

6. Before your 18th birthday, was a biological parent...ever lost to you through divorce, abandonment, or other reason?

7. Before your 18th birthday, was your mother or stepmother... often or very often pushed, grabbed, slapped, or had something thrown at her? Or sometimes, often, or very often kicked, bitten, hit with a fist, or hit with something hard? Or ever repeatedly hit over at least a few minutes or threatened with a gun or knife?

8. Before your 18th birthday, did you...live with anyone who was a problem drinker or alcoholic, or who used street drugs?

9. Before your 18th birthday, was a household member... depressed or mentally ill, or did a household member attempt suicide?

10. Before your 18th birthday, did a household member...go to prison?

How to Relax

Breathe—Starting in the lower abdomen, fill your lungs to capacity very slowly to the count of six, breathing through the nose. Hold for two. Breathe out slowly. To the count of eight, breathe out slowly through a very small hole between your lips, as if you're breathing through a tiny straw. Some even use a coffee-stirrer-type straw. Do this 10 to 12 times in a row. Don't rush it; you could hyperventilate.

Use systematic relaxation—This works with breathing. First, tense the muscles for six counts while inhaling. Hold for two.

Then release while exhaling for eight counts. Use the following sequence: Right foot, right lower leg and foot, entire right leg, left foot, left lower leg and foot, entire left leg, right hand, right forearm and hand, entire right arm, left hand, left forearm and hand, entire left arm, abdomen, chest, neck and shoulders.

THE POST-TRAUMATIC GROWTH INVENTORY

Key:

1 = I did not experience this change as a result of my crisis.

2 = I experienced this change to a very small degree as a result of my crisis.

3 = I experienced this change to a small degree as a result of my crisis.

4 = I experienced this change to a moderate degree as a result of my crisis.

5 = I experienced this change to a great degree as a result of my crisis.

6 = I experienced this change to a very great degree as a result of my crisis.

1. My priorities about what is important in life

   1
   2
   3
   4

5
6

2. I'm more likely to try to change things that need changing

    1
    2
    3
    4
    5
    6

3. An appreciation for the value of my own life

    1
    2
    3
    4
    5
    6

4. A feeling of self-reliance

    1
    2
    3
    4
    5
    6

5. A better understanding of spiritual matters

    1
    2

3

4

5

6

6. Knowing that I can count on people in times of trouble

1

2

3

4

5

6

7. A sense of closeness with others

1

2

3

4

5

6

8. Knowing I can handle difficulties

1

2

3

4

5

6

9. A willingness to express my emotions

1
2
3
4
5
6

10. Being able to accept the way things work out

   1
   2
   3
   4
   5
   6

11. Appreciating each day

   1
   2
   3
   4
   5
   6

12. Having compassion for others

   1
   2
   3
   4
   5
   6

13. I'm able to do better things with my life

    1

    2

    3

    4

    5

    6

14. New opportunities are available which wouldn't have been otherwise

    1

    2

    3

    4

    5

    6

15. Putting effort into my relationships

    1

    2

    3

    4

    5

    6

16. I have a stronger religious faith

    1

    2

    3

    4

5

6

17. I discovered that I'm stronger than I thought I was

    1

    2

    3

    4

    5

    6

18. I learned a great deal about how wonderful people are

    1

    2

    3

    4

    5

    6

19. I developed new interests

    1

    2

    3

    4

    5

    6

20. I accept needing others

    1

    2

3
4
5
6

21. I establish a new path for my life

1
2
3
4
5
6

Developed by Tedeschi and Calhoun

SYSTEMS OF ABUSE

SYSTEMS OF ABUSE

A core mindset of **power** drives all 12 forms of abuse.

POWER

1 DELUSIONS OF GRANDEUR
Believes they're smarter, wiser, stronger, more powerful than they really are.

2 ENTITLED
Acts as if others should give way to their preferences, or take care of their needs.

3 CREATES CHAOS
Gains control by turning people against each other.

4 RIGID RELIGION
Dictates belief system for everyone in the household.

5 CREDIT HOG
Steals other people's ideas, doesn't share the glory.

6 SUPREMACIST
Looks down on culture, color, gender, age, status -- thinks own identity is superior.

7 OBSESSED W/ RESPECT
May get aggressive to peers, children, elderly, who act with perceived disrespect.

8 FIXATED ON APPEARANCE
Expects others to keep secrets, maintain glossy public image regardless of reality.

LEARN MORE @SARAHMCDUGAL

SYSTEMS OF ABUSE-1

A core mindset of **power** drives all 12 forms of abuse.

CHILDREN

1 THREATS
Threatens to harm children, or actually harms them, if you don't do what they say.

2 MONEY
Doesn't pay child support, avoids reporting income, argues over legitimate needs.

3 SHAMING
Belittles you in front of the children, shames you or them by comparing your faults, undermines house rules and healthy parenting.

4 SILENCING
Leverages the children to keep you silent about other things, and makes you feel you can't speak out.

5 MOLESTATION
Abuses other people's children, even if they never overtly harm your own kids.

6 FEAR
Scares you in front of the kids, or hurts you in front of kids to scare them.

SYSTEMS OF ABUSE-2

A core mindset of **power** drives all 12 forms of abuse.

CULTURAL

1 MISTREATS YOU

and then blames it on either their cultural expectations, or yours. Or says its just how things were done in their family of origin.

2 DEMEANS YOU

because of your heritage, whether ethnicity, your language, your skin color, or your religious background.

3 FORCES YOU

to embrace their culture and heritage at the expense of your own, says theirs is better than yours, refuses to let you celebrate your own customs.

4 ISOLATES YOU

from mainstream cultural practices, and keeps you away from friends or activities that aren't rooted in their culture. Uses language barriers to prevent your socialization.

5 SILENCES YOU

by using cultural expectations or family shame to keep secrets, avoid friendships, or do things their way.

6 EXPLOITS YOU

by using language barriers to prevent your socialization and interaction with others.

SYSTEMS OF ABUSE-3

A core mindset of **power** drives all 12 forms of abuse.

EMOTIONAL

1 INVALIDATES

your perception of reality, your feelings, and your grasp of what happens around you.

2 INSULTS

you and then laughs it off and says "I was just joking! Why are you so sensitive?!"

3 DENIES

healthy non-sexual affection, gives you the silent treatment, or refuses to communicate about conflicts.

4 MANIPULATES

using false guilt, so that you feel guilty for things you didn't even say or do.

5 FLIPS ARGUMENTS

right back onto you and suddenly you're not talking about the real issue anymore, because you're both focused on why you reacted instead.

6 ACTS POSSESSIVE

but excuses it by calling it "protectiveness", and then making you feel horrible for trying to be independent

7 VACILLATES

creating an emotional rollercoaster so you're always braced for the other shoe to drop.

LEARN MORE @SARAHMCDUGAL

SYSTEMS OF ABUSE-4

A core mindset of **power** drives all 12 forms of abuse.

FINANCIAL

1 LIMITS
your access to money, accounts, income, cash flow, activities, shopping, travel, or any of the above.

2 TRACKS
every penny you spend, or expects you to track it and report back. May also include tracking gas mileage, grocery budget, and personal items.

3 DODGES
child support payments, shared parenting expenses, bill collectors, promised expenditures.

4 SPENDS
impulsively on themselves while micromanaging others in the family, or offsets stinginess with big gifts.

5 INTERFERES
with your access or eligibility for welfare, state aid, health care, scholarships, or other supports.

6 DECIDES
all the big financial things, without giving your opinion equal weight, sharing important details, or accounting for your needs.

7 LIES
about what they spend, where they spend it, or who they spend it with.

SYSTEMS OF ABUSE-5

A core mindset of **power** drives all 12 forms of abuse.

INTELLECTUAL

1 DEMANDS

perfection from you, your children, and possibly others around them. rooted in a need to reflect well back on them.

2 INSISTS

that you prove you have a right to hold an opinion, or that you show proof that your opinion is valid.

3 INSULTS

your education level, your intellect, your thinking ability, etc. Feels they and others are superior to you.

4 DUMBS

you down. acts surprised if you have something intelligent to say, assumes your comprehension level is lower than reality.

5 INTIMIDATED

by your brain. flummoxed by your mind. can't handle it if you speak intelligently for fear it will steal their limelight. May say you're boring.

6 REFUSES

to allow you the freedom to disagree or hold a contrary opinion to theirs, especially in public.

7 INVALIDATES

others if anyone notices their behaviors, abuses, or inconsistencies and begins to point it out.

SYSTEMS OF ABUSE-6

A core mindset of **power** drives all 12 forms of abuse.

PETS+STUFF

1 CONFISCATES

your car keys, your Driver's License, your passport or other identification, to "keep it safe" so you are trapped.

2 DAMAGES

your automobile, or refuses to keep it safely maintained and fueled, limiting your freedom and safety.

3 TRASHES

your favorite things, says "It was an accident." Or they go missing without explanation, and they hid it.

4 HARMS

your pets, or gives them away, or refuses to provide food and care for them when needed.

5 PUNCHES

walls, slams doors, breaks things, throws things, wreaks havoc, makes you afraid.

6 THREATENS

to do any of the above, even if they don't follow through on the threat for whatever reason.

187

SYSTEMS OF ABUSE-7

A core mindset of power drives all 12 forms of abuse.

PHYSICAL

1 RECKLESS
driving, road rage, bursts of anger or aggression towards others who are slower, weaker, less competent.

2 DISTURBS
your sleep and quiet times, wakes you from slumber, prevents you from resting by arguing, calling, texting, or making noise.

3 CHOKES
you (even once!), restrains you in any way, attempts to control your breath or freedom to breathe

4 BLOCKS
your exits, won't let you leave the room or the house, prevents you from calling for help.

5 PREVENTS
your access to medical care, emergency care, or appropriate medications, remedies, or nutrition.

6 HURTS
you by using items other than hands, whether implements or household things.

7 ASSAULTS
you by throwing things, slapping, hitting, spitting, punching, biting, pinching, kicking, or using body weight.

LEARN MORE @SARAHMCDUGAL

189

SYSTEMS OF ABUSE-8

A core mindset of **power** drives all 12 forms of abuse.

PSYCHOLOGICAL

1 GASLIGHTS

you by saying or doing things, even right in front of you, and then denying it later and making you question your sanity.

2 TERRORIZES

you, and then expects you to move on as if the incident or argument never happened.

3 CONTROLS

even the smallest aspects in your life - food, fun, friends - perhaps saying it's because they care so much.

4 PROJECTS

responsibility for their additions or compulsive behaviors onto others or saying it's your fault too.

5 DISPLAYS

weapons as a way to keep you aware of how they could hurt you if they really wanted to.

6 CONVINCES

you that they know much better than you do, and you should let them make decisions for you.

7 THREATENS

to hurt themselves, hurt others, kill themselves, kill others. Or brings these things up in a joking way.

A core mindset of **power** drives all 12 forms of abuse.

SEXUAL

1 FORCES

you to have sex. Coerces or urges you against your wishes. Or withholds sex as punishment for periods of time.

2 CRITICIZES

your body, your sexuality, or your sexual preferences. Shames or mocks your comfort zone.

3 DEMANDS

sexual favors as payment or compensation, in return for things they did or bought for you.

4 WATCHES

pornography or makes you watch it. Porn is inextricably tied to the human trafficking trade, and directly impacts reduced empathy.

5 CHEATS

on you by having affairs or one night stands, or by paying for sexual services. Or threatens to do these.

6 DISCONNECTS

from your heart, soul, and mind, lacking intimacy or connection beyond sexual acts.

7 MOLESTS

or sexually abuses others, regardless of whether adults or minors, outside your marriage.

193

SYSTEMS OF ABUSE-10

A core mindset of **power** drives all 12 forms of abuse.

SOCIAL

1 EAVESDROPS

on your communication and invades your privacy by monitoring your phone, email, messages, texts.

2 TRACKS

your social media accounts, posts, and interactions. Wants your passwords to be shared.

3 MONITORS

your mileage and always needs to know where you went, who you went with, and for how long.

4 DISCOURAGES

you from cultivating friendships, social interactions, healthy work connections, or fun times unless they are behind it.

5 DICTATES

your freedom or your options for pursuing education, employment, or self-improvement opportunities. Makes you ask permission to get involved with activities.

6 KEEPS

you at home as much as possible, where you are less influenced by other people's ways of thinking and doing things.

LEARN MORE @SARAHMCDUGAL

SYSTEMS OF ABUSE-11

A core mindset of **power** drives all 12 forms of abuse.

SPIRITUAL

1 TWISTS

Scriptures to avoid accountability, create power vacuum, or lord it over others around them.

2 EXPLOITS

religious beliefs and philosophies to gain advantage over others, or reduce obligations.

3 LEVERAGES

spiritual leaders, books, or information against you to get you to adhere to their preferences.

4 SILENCES

you with bible verses to teach subjugation, and condition you to accept their power over you.

5 BELIEVES

you need them in order to properly understand truth, communicate with God, or listen to the Holy Spirit.

6 SOUL

destroying behaviors of any kind that reduce your personhood, remove your voice, or come between you and your personal relationship with God.

SYSTEMS OF ABUSE-12

A core mindset of **power** drives all 12 forms of abuse.

VERBAL

1 DETAILS
how you should do everything, and makes sure you are told if you didn't do it their way to their satisfaction.

2 CUTS OFF
your opportunities to speak, or habitually interrupts you during conversation as if you add no value.

3 PUTS DOWN
your perspective, opinion, experience, knowledge, or ways of viewing things.

4 FORBIDS
you from talking to others about issues, or confiding in trusted friends or mentors when needed.

5 SHAMES
you, silences you, insults you, and communicates that they have a low opinion of your worth.

6 YELLS
at you, screams, swears, calls you names or uses tones of voice that are condescending and sarcastic.

7 HUMILIATES
you by treating you in these ways in front of others, or encouraging other people to treat you this way too.

LOVE & HONOR WHEEL

Love & Honor Wheel

CHILD

- Protects children physically and emotionally
- Treats children with kindness and patience
- Builds you up in front of your children
- Models honesty at home and in public
- Provides consistent financial stability

CULTURE

- Embraces the best of both your cultures
- Uplifts what you love about your own culture
- Shows sensitivity to other cultural practices
- Supports your language learning and cultural adaptation

LOVE & HONOR

- Acknowledges reality without evasion
- Admits past events transparently
- Accepts personal responsibility for actions
- Gives credit to those who have earned it
- Realizes own limitations and weaknesses
- Seeks mentorship and counseling
- Accepts accountability with humility
- Pursues recovery for any addictions
- Honors the value of others regardless of age, culture, gender, ethnicity
- Treats others with respect regardless of what they have to offer
- Seeks to serve others with selfless kindness
- Refuses to use power to exploit others

EMOTIONAL

- Validates your feelings
- Communicates honestly
- Takes responsibility for own actions
- Extends trust and independence
- Offers affection and safety

FINANCIAL

- Equal access to money
- Shared financial decisions and accounts
- No secret accounts, expenditures, or incomes
- Communicates with transparency about money
- Pays full child support on time

INTELLECTUAL

- Straightforward communication
- Supports your ideas
- Values your opinions
- Gives grace for your mistakes
- Appreciates your tastes
- Builds you up
- Trusts your judgment as a partner

PETS & PROPERTY

- Cares for pets kindly
- Treats property with respect
- Maintains your car
- Respects your belongings
- Does not interfere or threaten the things you own

VERBAL

- Uses words to build you up
- Honors you in front of others
- Speaks honestly and openly
- Gives genuine compliments, not flattery
- Delights in your conversation
- Encourages you to speak truth to others
- Avoids raised voice or silent treatment

SPIRITUAL

- Soul-enriching behaviors
- Accepts Scripture's call to servant leadership
- Refuses to seek power over you
- Encourages your spiritual connection
- Respects your choice of counselors
- Seeks shared spiritual growth without control

SOCIAL

- Encourages your friendships
- Engages with your family connections
- Respects your right to privacy
- Appreciates your talents
- Supports your desires to work/study
- Ensures equal access to social activities

SEXUAL

- Gives genuine intimacy
- Offers sexual affection without strings
- Refuses to view pornography
- Appreciates your body
- Remains sexually faithful
- Respects when you're not in the mood

PSYCHOLOGICAL

- Admits own mistakes
- Keeps weapons locked up
- Does not threaten to harm self or others
- Honestly accepts reality
- Respects your identity
- Does not rewrite history

PHYSICAL

- Drives safely and responsibly
- Treats your body with respect
- Touches you gently
- Protects you from pain
- Supports your right to free choice
- Offers non-sexual affection without strings

203

SEXUAL ADDICTION RECOVERY

If the spell of sexual addiction is to be broken, all the energy, time, and resources that have been invested in the addiction must now be invested in recovery. The weekly schedule must be organized around recovery, with the components of the program displacing the addictive activity, pushing it out of the person's life completely. The best sexual addiction recovery programs look like this:

- Weekly counseling
- Group meetings once to seven times per week
- Filtering on all devices
- Weekly session with an accountability partner or sponsor
- Corporate worship and fellowship
- Bibliotherapy (reading material)
- Personal devotions

1. Counseling—Weekly counseling with a counselor who understands addictions and has a good reputation for treating them is essential. Abide Counseling Network (abidecounseling.com) offers Adventist-informed, biblical mental health counseling and coaching via telephone and

internet. If one wishes for a face-to-face counselor, it may be helpful to search the Psychology Today database, which will yield mostly non-Christian options, but some Christian/biblical options. A directory of Seventh-day Adventist counselors can be found at the NAD Family Life website (nadfamily.org, click on "Resources" and "Directory of Counselors.") Some other groups that have counselor directories are the American Association of Christian Counselors (connect.aacc.net) and New Life Live (newlife.com/counselors).

2. Group Meetings—Weekly, twice-weekly, or even more frequent group counseling with a group that helps people in addiction is also essential. There are several 12-step groups that address sexual addiction in a non-religious yet biblically-based way. Celebrate Recovery comes from a more openly Christian perspective with a very well-run and comprehensive, no-cost program based on the Beatitudes (celebraterecovery.com). Pure Desire (puredesire.org) uses a step approach based on the Proverbs. Sexual Addicts Anonymous (saa-recovery.org/meetings/) offers some teleconferencing options. Harvest USA (harvestusa.org) has discipleship ministries for men and women in sexual addiction. Small Groups Online (smallgroupsonline.org) offers a variety of group support options for a small fee.

3. Filtering on All Devices—Filtering all devices must take place. Let's face it, screens are dangerous to an addict. Digital-age intimacy and relationship expert Robert Weiss recommends Net Nanny, Qustodio, Web Watcher, and Covenant Eyes. They all function differently, with options such as forwarding browsing history to an accountability partner. We must avoid as much temptation as possible, and then resist it

when we can't avoid it. Net filters are an important temptation-avoiding strategy.

4. Accountability Partner or Sponsor—Besides a personal counselor, the addict in recovery benefits from an accountability partner who will oversee all the components of the program and hold the addict accountable for compliance. We're told to "Confess your sins to one another, and pray for one another so that you may be healed" (James 5:16, NASB). We don't confess to another as a mediator between ourselves and God, as only Jesus plays that role (1 Timothy 2:5). But sharing our struggle and failures with a trusted human being can provide a needed reality check and can help wake us up to the heinousness of sin. Twelve-step programs use sponsors for accountability, but the sponsee often must reach out to the sponsor. We shouldn't be afraid to ask others to help in this capacity, but it can be helpful to tell them exactly what it would require, for instance, "Can you act as my accountability partner by chatting on the phone twice a week for ten minutes about how I'm doing with my recovery program?"

5. Corporate Worship and Fellowship—Church attendance or other spiritually uplifting social engagements will provide a source of connection whereby basic love and social needs can be met. While some churches' toxicity may be so extreme as to be contraindicated for healing, most have at least some godly, functional members with whom we can connect.

6. Bibliotherapy—Reading books on addiction recovery can make a huge difference by changing our headspace from one of addiction to one of recovery.

Reading ideas:

Addiction and Grace by Harold May

At the Altar of Sexual Idolatry by Steve Gallagher

Celebrate Recovery Participants Guides

Finally Free by Heath Lambert

Healing the Wounds of Sexual Addiction by Mark R. Laaser

Healing the Broken Brain by Elden Chalmers

Ministry of Healing by Ellen White

Out of the Shadows: Understanding Sexual Addiction by Patrick Carnes

Overcoming Porn by Mike Phillips

Sexual Detox: A Guide for Guys Who Are Sick of Porn by Tim Challies

The Fight of Your Life: Manning Up to the Challenge of Sexual Integrity by Tim Clinton

The Journey to Wholeness by Adventist Recovery Ministries

The Twelve Steps for Christians

Your Sexually Addicted Spouse by Dr Barbara Steffens and Marsha Means

7. Personal Devotions—Daily Bible study and prayer will assist in the process of mind and thought healing, bringing the thoughts out of the gutter of depraved sensuality into the invigorating air of purity and principle. It will warm the heart with the news of a God who loves us as we are but also leads us on from there into a better life.

Can God restore our self-respect, relationships, self-control, moral conscience, health, sanity, and spirituality? I'll let Paul answer: "Now to Him who is able to do exceedingly abundantly above all that we ask or think, according to the power that works in us, to Him be glory in the church by Christ Jesus to all generations, forever and ever. Amen" (Ephesians 3:20-21).

ABOUT THE AUTHORS

Sarah McDugal is an author, speaker, trainer and abuse recovery coach who works exclusively with women wounded by toxic relationships in the faith community. She emphasizes biblical prevention, responsible strategy, and wholistic healing in her appearances on podcasts, TV, radio, training events and lectures. An alumnus of Southern Adventist University, she also earned her Master's Degree in International Development from Andrews University. She is the author of *One Face: Shed the Mask, Own Your Values, and Lead Wisely* (2016), and co-author of *Myths We Believe, Predators We Trust: 37 Things You Don't Want to Know About Abuse in Church (But You Really Should)* (2019).

Sarah serves on the nationwide #EndItNow Task Force for policy on sexual ethics and misconduct in the faith community. A former clergy spouse, she worked for twenty years in branding and media production, resource development, and ministerial spouse support. In addition to training churches and organizations on practical ways to better respond to abuse, Sarah provides coaching on clarity and emotional recovery, and offers situational consulting for churches facing abuse issues. In 2017 Sarah founded WILD, offering individual and group coaching packages, online training courses, confidential peer support groups, and a membership coaching community. *www.wildernesstowild.com*

Jennifer Jill Schwirzer graduated with a Master of Science in Human Services with a specialization in Mental Health Counseling from Capella University in 2008 and holds a counseling license in the state of Florida. She passed both the National Certified Counselor (NCC) exam and the National Clinical Mental Health Counseling Exam (NCMHCE) through the National Board for Certified Counselors (NBCC).

Jennifer runs a private counseling practice out of her home office in Orlando, Florida, and is the director of Abide Counseling Network. She also hosts *A Multitude of Counselors*, a 3ABN program focusing on mental health issues.

Nicole Parker holds a Master's in Pastoral Ministry and is an adjunct faculty member in the School of Religion at Southern Adventist University, teaching Biblical Counseling and co-teaching Sexuality and Scripture with her husband, Dr. Alan Parker.

She is an international speaker on emotional healing and wholeness, healing from abuse, practical spirituality, and marriage. Nicole authored *Tales of the Exodus*, a series of best-selling children's books bringing the sanctuary message to life for all ages.

Together, Sarah, Jennifer, and Nicole co-founded the Bucket Brigade Against Abuse, a non-profit created to meet the overwhelming need to guide sexual abuse victims to safely report, and to train spiritual leaders in how to better recognize and respond to abuse in the church.

NOTES

2. Trauma and the Path Forward

1. American Psychiatric Association, *Diagnostic and statistical manual of mental disorders* (5th ed.).
2. Vincent Felitti, "The Origins of Addiction: Evidence from the Adverse Childhood Experiences Study," Kaiser Permanente Medical Care Program, p. 11.
3. Sherry Peters, "Who Needs to Pay Attention to the ACE Study?" Georgetown University Center for Child and Human Development, p. 1.
4. Daoud Hari, *The Translator*, p. 79.
5. Lawrence Calhoun, Personal email correspondence, July 12, 2018.
6. Kay Wilson, "I Believe with an Imperfect Faith," *Blogs: The Times of Israel*.

3. Forgiving Without Enabling

1. Ty Gibson, @tyfgibson, tweeted.

4. Victim, Survivor, Thriver, Defender

1. Ellen White, *Patriarchs and Prophets*, p. 33.
2. Ellen White, *The Desire of Ages*, p. 22.
3. Tim Clinton, *The God Attachment*, p. 77.

5. Identifying Perpetrators

1. Gavin de Becker, foreword of *Predators* by Anna Salter, pg. ix.
2. RAINN, *About Sexual Assault,* https://www.rainn.org/about-sexual-assault.
3. Howard N. Snyder, *Sexual Assault of Young Children as Reported to*

Law Enforcement, p.2, retrieved from https://www.bjs.gov/content/pub/pdf/saycrle.pdf.

4. Dr. Gene Abel, *The Child Abuser: How Can You Spot Him?*, Redbook, 100 (1987, August) retrieved from https://www.zeroabuseproject.org/victim-assistance/jwrc/keep-kids-safe/sexual-offenders-101/sexuality-of-offenders/.

5. Gavin de Becker, foreword of *Predators* by Anna C. Salter, pg. x.

6. Cory Jewell and Steve Jenson, *Understanding and Protecting Your Children from Child Molesters and Predators,* Oprah.com.

7. David Finkelhor and Sharon Araji, "Explanations of Pedophilia: A Four Factor Model." *The Journal of Sex Research*, vol. 22, no. 2, 1986, pp. 145–161. *JSTOR*, www.jstor.org/stable/3812437.

8. Anna C. Salter, *Predators,* pg 5.

9. Anna C. Salter, *Predators,* pg 5.

10. Jimmy Hinton, *Why I Talk about Abusers "Testing" Instead of Grooming*, JimmyHinton.org.

11. Jimmy Hinton, *Abusers Look for Opportunities More than Vulnerabilities*, JimmyHinton.org.

12. Anna C. Salter, *Predators,* pg 20.

13. Anna C. Salter, *Predators,* pg 25.

6. Defenders as Healers

1. Ellen White, *Education,* p. 57.

2. Sarah McDugal, *Systems of Abuse vs Love and Honor,* http://sarahmcdugal.com/abuse-wheel/

3. Gandolf and Russel. The Case Against Anger Management for Batterers, https://www.biscmi.org/wp-content/uploads/2015/05/THE-CASE-AGAINST-Anger-control-for-batterers.pdf, accessed October 27, 2019.

7. When Abuse Comes to Church

1. David Lisak, et al., "False Allegations of Sexual Assault: An Analysis of Ten Years of Reported Cases" *Violence Against Women,* p. 1318-1334.

2. Jennifer Truman, et al., "Criminal Victimization, 2013" *Bureau of Justice Statistics.*

3. A. Moller et al., "Tonic Immobility During Sexual Assault: A Common

Reaction Predicting Post-Traumatic Stress Disorder and Severe Depression" *Acta Obstetrics and Gynecology, Scandinavia,* p. 932-938.
4. PBS.org "No Safe Place: Rape and Sexual Assault."
5. Ellen White, *Patriarchs and Prophets,* p. 725.
6. Psalm 82 Initiative.

9. Discerning Genuine Repentance

1. Ellen White, *The Desire of Ages,* p. 712.

Made in the USA
Columbia, SC
14 March 2021